A Dressmaker's Threads

Also by Evelyn Lerman

Safer Sex: The New Morality

Teen Moms: The Pain and the Promise

A Dressmaker's Threads:

The Life and the Legacy
of
My Russian Immigrant Mother

By

Evelyn Lerman

AuthorHouse™
1663 Liberty Drive
Bloomington, IN 47403
www.authorhouse.com
Phone: 1-800-839-8640

Published by AuthorHouse   03/27/2013

ISBN: 978-1-4817-3500-1 (sc)
ISBN: 978-1-4817-3499-8 (e)

Library of Congress Control Number: 2013905616

Contents

Civia is Born, 1898; Civia 1898-1902; At Home in the
Pale of Settlement; Barsha's Death, 1902; Civia 1902-
1908; Apprenticeship in the Shtetl, 1909-1917; Meyer
Comes to Work for Chaim, 1910; Meyer's Travels,
1910; The Wedding, July 25, 1918; Escape, 1919;
Travel to America, 1919-1920; Ellis Island, 1920

A Dressmaker's Threads

Genealogy

Meyer Gorfinkel
12/25/1897-8/15/1953
Civia Elkind
8/25/1898-1/2/1974
m. 7/25/1918

Miriam Irene Gorfinkel
b.7/28/1919-d.9/13/2003
Ray Levine
d.4/10/1965
Hyman Lockwood
b.8/15/1916-d.7/12/1966

Blossom Gorfinkel
b.10/8/1921-d.12/22/1993
David Chiller
b.8/6/1914-d.9/9/2007
m. 7/201945

Evelyn Gorfinkel
b.12/23/1925
Albert Lerman
b.1/30/1925
m.6/22/1947

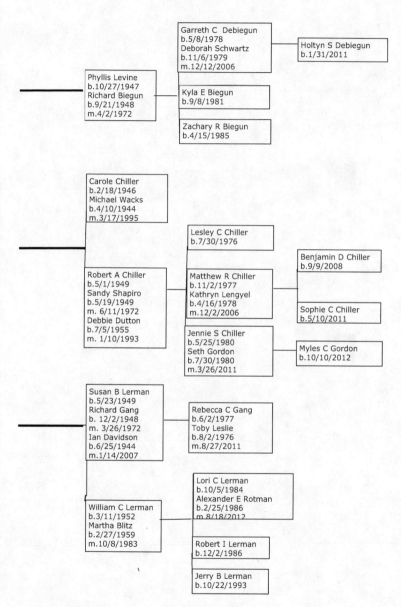

Garreth C Debiegun
b.5/8/1978
Deborah Schwartz
b.11/6/1979
m.12/12/2006

Holtyn S Debiegun
b.1/31/2011

Phyllis Levine
b.10/27/1947
Richard Biegun
b.9/21/1948
m.4/2/1972

Kyla E Biegun
b.9/8/1981

Zachary R Biegun
b.4/15/1985

Carole Chiller
b.2/18/1946
Michael Wacks
b.4/10/1944
m.3/17/1995

Lesley C Chiller
b.7/30/1976

Benjamin D Chiller
b.9/9/2008

Robert A Chiller
b.5/1/1949
Sandy Shapiro
b.5/19/1949
m. 6/11/1972
Debbie Dutton
b.7/5/1955
m. 1/10/1993

Matthew R Chiller
b.11/2/1977
Kathryn Lengyel
b.4/16/1978
m.12/2/2006

Sophie C Chiller
b.5/10/2011

Jennie S Chiller
b.5/25/1980
Seth Gordon
b.7/30/1980
m.3/26/2011

Myles C Gordon
b.10/10/2012

Susan B Lerman
b.5/23/1949
Richard Gang
b. 12/2/1948
m. 3/26/1972
Ian Davidson
b.6/25/1944
m.1/14/2007

Rebecca C Gang
b.6/2/1977
Toby Leslie
b.8/2/1976
m.8/27/2011

Lori C Lerman
b.10/5/1984
Alexander E Rotman
b.2/25/1986
m.8/18/2012

William C Lerman
b.3/11/1952
Martha Blitz
b.2/27/1959
m.10/8/1983

Robert I Lerman
b.12/2/1986

Jerry B Lerman
b.10/22/1993

Acknowledgments

It takes a loving family and loyal friends to help an author give birth to a book. I have many people to thank, so please forgive me if your name doesn't appear, and know that I cherish every interaction, every discussion, every suggestion, and every insight you gave me as I stumbled and faltered. Know that it was because of each of you that I finally succeeded in finishing *The Dressmaker's Threads.* My mother would have been proud of all of us.

With heartfelt thanks to . . .

My loving husband Allie for his patience, forbearance, editorial wisdom and computer assistance.

My daughter Susan who took time out of her eighty-hour work week to read and edit my book.

My granddaughter Lori for the camp pictures and the tender editing which made every error seem a blessing.

My nephew Robert for his treasure trove of old family pictures.

My son Bill for his endless cheerleading and his fine-tuned ear for editing the Maine dialect.

My friends Carol and Sam for their wonderful photography.

My granddaughter Rebecca for so willingly lending me her writer's ear.

My friend Suki who, from her first reading of "The Needle" twenty years ago, encouraged me to write the book.

My friends/colleagues in the Writers' Club for listening, critiquing, and valuing my writing.

My new friends, Marilyn Simpson and Pati Lindsay, for their careful editing.

. . . and to my dear friend Jeanne Warren Lindsay, who published my two earlier books but is now retiring, yet gave unstintingly of her energy, expertise and advice.

Glossary —
Yiddish to English

A clug to Columbus: A pox on Columbus for discovering America (used when the children were being too American).

American mishugas: American foolishness.

B'rachah: Prayer.

Babele: Diminutive for baby, her youngest child.

Bar Mitzvah: The religious rite of passage for 13-year-old boys, conducted in the Shul.

Bassinkeh: Yiddish diminutive for Blossom.

Besser: Better.

By meer bish du schein: To me you are beautiful.

Chutzpadich: Full of chutzpah, full of gall.

Coureveh: Prostitute.

Daven: To pray in Orthodox Shul. This is accompanied by swaying back and forth.

Dimel: A dime.

Drei kinder: Three children.

Du kenst nit weizen a naar a halbeh arbet: You can't show a fool work half done.

Ess, mine kinder: Eat, my children.

Fagele: A small bird, connoting homosexuality.

Floomen mit kartofle: Prunes with potatoes.

Gelt: Money.

Chanukah gelt: Money given on Chanukah.

Ghetto: The restricted area where Jews were required to live.

Goldene medinah: Golden Land, streets paved with gold.

Gootskeit: Goodness.

Gottenyu: My God, Our God.

Goyish: Very Gentile, like a Goy (Gentile).

Hehr ve ess schmecht: Hear how it smells.

Kaddish: Memorial service for the dead.

Kishkeh: Derma, meat-stuffed cow intestines.

Lichtich: Light of my life.

Mayerke: Yiddish diminutive for Meyer.

Meer es nicht: When you stop eating.

Mine kind: My child.

Minyan: The ten men needed to hold a religious service.

Mirele: Miriam, diminutive.

Mohliver: Yiddish name for Mogilev, the shtetl.

Moomah Sorah: Mother Sarah.

My Mun: My husband.

Noch Ne'ilah: After Ne'ilah. (Late in the Day of Atonement, when the gates to Heaven close, your time is up.)

Oy, vey!: Woe is me.

Pale of Settlement: A portion of the Soviet Union set aside for Jews.

Payot: Uncut sideburns worn by Orthodox Jews.

Plymutt: Plymouth automobile.

Pogrom: An assault on a Jewish shtetl, combining rape, killing, burning, stealing, frequently ordered by the government.

Poopek: The gizzard of a chicken.

Prostrate: Prostate cancer.

Ret uff Ivrit!: Speak in Hebrew!

Rov: Rabbi.

Schlepping: Lugging.

Schnapps: Liquor.

Shanda: A shame for the neighbors.

Shivah: Mourning for the dead.

Shtetl: A small village, generally in the Pale of Settlement.

Shul: Jewish Temple.

Tachrichim: Shrouds.

Talmud: Commentaries by learned Rabbis and other scholars on the Torah.

Tsveetochneechai: A Russian tea housed in a pirate's chest.

Tierer Gott: Dear God.

Timble: Thimble.

Torah: The five books of Moses, read from beginning to end every year in Shul.

Treds: Threads.

Tshchot: Abacus.

"Tyerer liebe Civia, dein bruder Abba is tait. Er hot geshtorben fum pneumonia laster voch.": "Dear beloved Civia: Your brother Abba is dead. He died from pneumonia last week."

Unter babele's vigele: Yiddish lullaby: Under the baby's crib stands a white onion; the onion will go out to bargain for raisins and almonds so the baby will grow up strong and healthy.

Yeshivah bochers: Boys who go to the Yeshivah, the Hebrew school.

Zee Shtait oof: She is standing up.

Zenitt: Zenith TV.

Dedicated to my Mother
Tzatzilia Yefimivna Elkind Gorfinkel
aka Lichtich, Civia, Ceil, Mrsa. G., Mamutchka, Nana
Ceil

The Shadow

I think I walk alone, but she is there
Supporting me, counseling me, consoling me.

An original thought seems familiar.
Instilled in me at the age of ten,

Brought to consciousness at any age.
Translated into English from the Yiddish,

There for me to remember
To adapt to any circumstance.

What do we leave when we leave?
If we are bountiful enough, perhaps a shadow.

June, 2012, in Maine. Ev and Allie's 65th anniversary year.

Introduction

December 23, 2000. I chose today to start this book about my mother, although I have been writing about her for many years. I'm 75 years old today, the age she was when she died. That makes me feel it's the right time to gather her stories together because perhaps now I can see life better through her eyes, Since I have to explain this to you, I know I haven't come to terms with it yet, for it seems "chutzpahdik" to try to tell her story. I have never suffered the way she did, I have never had to work as hard as she did, and surely I don't have her wit, the Russian Jewish accent, her carriage, her boundless enthusiasm for life, her intensity of feeling for everything she touched, and the passion of her love for us, her three children.

But, I'm not saying I'm worthless. Not at all. As the youngest of her daughters, I was the one she showered with compliments. I was so smart, so beautiful, so loved, so talented. No one could come close to me; that's how special I felt I was in my mother's eyes. I laughed when she carried on, and brushed it aside. "You're my mother," I'd scoff. "How can you be so sure I am so special?"

She'd laugh. "I just know, Babele," she'd smile with those tiny, straight, white teeth glowing. "My baby is wonderful."

Even as I blew it away, some of it stuck, for though I'm not in the galaxy she invented for me, I do feel competent, comfortable in my own skin, and truly not afraid of much. But I admit I am a little afraid of starting this book. I so want to do her justice, and I so want the reader to see what made her so special. I'd love the reader to say, "This is not just another mother story. This one is worth reading." If you pick it up and read it, and if you find my mother just as fascinating as I did, and if you agree with my friends who, every time I told them a story about her, said, "Write it, Ev," just send me an e-mail at lerman.evelyn@gmail.com. Of course, if you don't do any of the above, or if you find it boring, you still have the right to let me know that. She made me strong enough to accept criticism, but I'll prefer the love letters, being human after all.

December 23, 2007. I'm now seven years older than my mother was when she died, and am still writing stories about her, and have not yet put them together in a book. But this year something special happened in the Monday morning writing class I teach at the University of South Florida. It's a class at the Academy for Lifelong Learning, where seniors like me teach and take classes. We write together, we share our stories, we critique for each other, and we work at home to bring new pieces to school to read aloud. This year two Mondays fell on holidays, so we had a three-week vacation between classes.

"Prepare to write the story you've always wanted to write," I told them. "Get your ideas together, choose a theme, and come to class ready to share your plans."

As soon as it was out of my mouth, I wanted to choke it back. Would I finally have to confront my anxieties, gather all my stories together, and make the commitment to write this book? "You can't give the assignment and not do it" is my teaching philosophy, so the deed is done. I'm on my way.

June 22, 2012. Here I am again, five years later, and this time it's for real. It's for real because as my dear husband and I were packing for our summer in Maine, he said, "Darling, this is the last year I am schlepping your books to Maine. Either you write this year or never."

He was referring to my journals, all fifty of them, those I have been writing since I was a young woman. They are heavy, filling three sturdy milk cartons, and increasingly heavier as both of us get older and older. I agreed. The time has come to write her story, and to pull together the threads of her legacy.

Civia in Russia

Prologue

This story will be a mixture of my memories and all those I have pried loose from my sisters, my children and their cousins, my grandchildren and their cousins, and the extended family and friends who knew her and whose lives were touched by her. Mother never told her complete story to any of us, so the missing parts will be based on research of the periods when she lived in Russia as a child, escaped during the Bolshevik Revolution in 1917, and came to America with a sick husband and infant daughter in 1919. I use quotation marks for conversations I actually heard and a double hyphen (--) for conversations I made up, based on my knowledge of the people and times involved.

I will also tell the story of her legacy: the love of education, the powerful work ethic, the love of and loyalty to family, the optimistic attitude, the joy in living that she passed on to her children, her grandchildren and even her great-grandchildren. I am older than she was when she died so I thought perhaps now I could see the family through her eyes. But age alone is not enough to give me her perspective and her vision. I am the spoiled child of a loving, devoted mother. In marriage I became the spoiled wife of a loving, devoted husband. I crawled from her bed into his with complete innocence. Of course he would love me as she did, I was her babele, the youngest who could do no wrong. My self-image is strong and I am not afraid of much that my mind and my emotions can conquer.

She loved education, her work as a dressmaker, her customers and her three children above all. She loved Coolidge Corner (she called it Coolidge's Corner), and the way the beloved sun (der lieber zun) shone into her front window as she worked at her machine. "Oy," she said one day, "they are taking down the Church and Coolidge's Corner will never be the same." How right she was. The Episcopalian Church across the street was a majestic building towering over the corner of two streets just opposite her apartment building. It was the beginning of the end of the elegance of Coolidge Corner. That site became a gym, the quality of the stores changed, and Ceil's own apartment was cut into two so the landlord could collect two rents instead of one. She missed the weddings and the funerals, watching the people come to "work out."

"Work out what?" she'd ask. "Work is work and gym is play." She'd sigh and continue her talk with God.

"I talk with God," she told me. "He helps me. I tell Him about my children, I tell Him I need to stay healthy so I can earn a living for them, educate them, and take care of my sick husband. I talk to God and He answers me."

I often ask myself if I believe in God. My questions cause me to marvel even more at her personal relationship with Him. I don't have it, but perhaps I don't need it as she did. I talk with my husband and together we resolve the questions we have. But she didn't have that relationship. She talked with God, with her children and with her customers. But with very personal issues she talked mostly with God.

"Talk is cheap," people say, but talk with Mrs. G. could be costly. She held court over her machine and people from what she called "all walks of life" sat with her while she worked. Saturdays were particularly busy at Mrs. G's Salon. She dispensed homegrown wisdom, a wonderful listening ear, fruit and tea, and sometimes charity. This charity was based on her unique pricing system. Considered one of the best dressmakers in the Boston/Brookline area, Mrs. G. was much sought after by ladies of fashion. Not working, they had lots of time to spend in her company, bringing their clothes from couturier shops and from Filene's Basement.

Her upper middle class customers knew she was expensive, and they also knew that if you asked her how much something was going to be, she would answer, "You can't know a job until you finish it." The smart ones were quiet after that, because the ones who pushed for the price found themselves getting less and less attention until they discovered they were no longer part of her customer group. "I weed 'em out," she told me. Her prices were high, but her work was excellent and her well-to-do customers were happy to have her. If sometimes they paid a little extra, that took care of the shop girls who lived in her building and who were barely getting by on their meager wages. "The Robber of Beacon Street" was the fond nickname some had for her, although "The Angel of Beacon Street" was not far behind. Her Robin Hood philosophy went along with her expansive personality.

"She's worth it," Mrs. Cohen would smile when Mrs. Abrams complained.

"She's a great fitter, she gives it to you on time, and

she's fun to be with. What else do you want?"

So when Elsie from upstairs came to pick up her dress for a friend's wedding and asked "How much?" Mrs. G. would hug her and say, "Don't worry. No charge, darling. Enjoy," and hand her the dress, beautifully pressed, in a new plastic garment bag.

Unwary Mrs. Green, the next customer half an hour later, would wince a little at the price.

"Oh, darling," said Mrs. G, "I needed to do two fittings, had to let it out a hair, evened off the hem, took a nip here and a tuck there, a smidgeon in the back, and it looks perfect. It's a bargain for the price. You look beautiful," and Mrs. Green would smile at herself in the mirror, pay my mother, and sit down for a chat.

"My husband is not paying enough attention to me, Mrs. G."

"Why wouldn't he, a lovely woman like you," Mrs. G. would beam. "Didn't he just give you a three-carat diamond ring you showed me?"

"He did, but the question is why did he do it? Is he guilty of something?"

"No, darling, he just works very hard and is tired when he comes home, but he comes home and he loves you. Here, have a cup of tea and a cookie. Hug him when he comes home. Tell him he is wonderful. Listen to his troubles. Scratch his back."

Mrs. Green would smile, "You're expensive, Mrs. G., but you're worth it."

One story up from the street she sat, high above Coolidge Corner, one flight to the landing at the first floor, another flight of marble stairs to her second floor apartment. From her observation post she watched people running for the streetcar, laughing to herself as they jumped aboard at the last minute, and sighing for them when they missed it and stamped their feet impatiently waiting for the next car. She watched mothers pushing baby carriages, elderly women pushing walkers, teenagers pushing bikes or jostling each other. If she saw someone just "killing time" she took personal offense. Patient in so many ways, she had no patience for people doing nothing. Killing time was a crime. "Let them take care of sick children," she'd say.

Her favorite scene on her Coolidge Corner stage was the Boston Marathon, held every year on Patriot's Day. This 26.2-mile run started in Hopkinton and leveled off at Coolidge Corner after struggling through Newton with its famous Heartbreak Hill where so many runners quit. By the time they got to Coolidge Corner it was easy to tell who the front-runners were. People were lined up four deep on the curb cheering the runners on, passing them oranges and cold drinks, and Mrs. G. was up in her perch smiling down on them all. But much as she loved the front runners who came through around 1 p.m., she saved her real love for the stragglers who walked by painfully at three or four in the afternoon, those with no hope of winning but a burning desire to finish. For these she would open the window and call down cheers, clapping, and telling them she was proud of them for finishing.

I never questioned an action or reaction of my mother's. They all seemed right to me. The underdog deserved her special attention. Now I have burning questions: Why did you marry my father? What did you think of sex? Tell me about your life with two stepmothers. What was life in Russia like when you were a little girl? Did the Bolsheviks hurt you? Were you afraid when you were coming to this country? What was it like to have a baby, a sick husband, and not speak the language? And more. But I didn't know then that I wanted to know these things and she didn't like to talk about life in the 'old country.'

"This is the goldene medina, the golden land. Life in Russia is over. Here is where we will be successful: you will go to college and be a professor; Bassinke will go to college and become a lawyer. Mirele will go to college and be a dietician. My girls have to have something to fall back on. You never know what can happen to a husband. Maybe he won't be able to support you and you need to be able to support yourself."

This in spite of my father mumbling in the background, "Girls don't need education, Lichtich. Tzivia, save your money for us. They will marry and have children and their husbands will support them. Don't waste your money on college for girls."

But my mother was determined. Her three girls, her drei kinder, would go to college and her husband would have to accept that. Meyer complained, but since she was the wage earner, he had no clout.

Poor daddy. When I was younger I never appreciated either him or the situation he was in. I only knew that he was sick with the asthma and arthritis he contracted in the Czar's Army and we girls had to take care of him unless he was away. Away meant he was either in the hospital to which the screaming ambulance had taken him or he was in Florida or Arizona. He liked the warm places to which he retreated when life became unbearable in Brookline. My mother sent him gladly so she could do her own thing and not have to justify her actions to him. She could spend money on her three girls and he couldn't complain. In warm climates his arthritis felt better and he didn't need to wear heavy clothing. He found other men to play cards with and he cooked his own meals, health food my mother couldn't tolerate. He bought medicines across the border in Mexico, trying every new remedy that came along. His illness made him a shadow father and husband while I was growing up.

Now that I am twenty-seven years older than he was when he died of kidney failure from all the medications he took, I realize that not only was he a good man, but a smart one as well. A reader, he devoured the *Boston Globe* and the *Jewish Forward*, which he read in Hebrew/Yiddish. This newspaper for the immigrant population kept him up to date on the anti-Semitism in Europe and the Socialist philosophy of the times. Like Daddy, it had a pinkish point of view and it fit into his worldview.

How different they were, my mother and father. She held herself like a Czarina, tall and stately, dreaming dreams of grandeur and building castles in the air. She thought of herself as a queen who just happened to be born a Jewish peasant. He was a realist, on top of the politics of the day, recognizing the roadblocks for Jews even in America. She talked to God and he expressed his disdain for religion by roasting a turkey on Yom Kippur, the day of fasting and atonement, and eating it all day as he went by the kitchen counter. She dreamed dreams of success and he faced daily issues of survival.

We had mother's extended family when we were young, but lost touch as the years went by. Mostly, I think this was because my mother was so good and she couldn't understand why her brothers and sister were so bad. Uncle Joe and Uncle Benny in Worcester, the uncles my parents worked for and my father hated, Uncle Harry in Worcester with his frail wife Sarah who bore him eight children, Uncle Dave who was married to a woman who had already had three husbands, Auntie Manya who looked like a witch and moved away to Chicago, and numerous cousins. By the time I was a teenager, Benny and Joe had divorced their wives and married their secretaries and the only two aunts I really loved, Anna and Esther, were not invited to family gatherings. Daddy's family never left Russia, and I know nothing about them because I never had the sense to ask.

On Sundays we'd drive to Worcester to visit, Daddy grumbling all the way about how awful Mother's family was, Mother agreeing, but saying they were our only family. We'd drive for what seemed forever down the Worcester Turnpike, Daddy at the wheel of the DeSoto, hat on top of his handsome head, mother sitting beside him in the front seat, and the three of us in the back. I believed with all of my six-year-old knowledge that if you wore a hat while you were driving, a policeman would pinch you, so I kept taking Daddy's hat off his head. Poor Daddy, I'd take it off and he'd put it back on. Off, on, off, on, the miracle being that we survived his driving and got to Worcester at all. The highlight of the trip was the stop at Hood's Farm in Wayland where they had cows who made not only cold, rich, wonderful milk, but also cold, rich, wonderful vanilla ice cream. The angels at the farm put that ice cream on top of freshly baked rich, chocolate frosted fudge cake, all on a large plate. We stopped there on our way to Uncle Harry's and Aunt Sarah's, and my fat, insatiable child's body quivered with joy each trip. Cholesterol and weight conscious now, that concoction is a no-no, but I've asked my loved ones, on the day that I am due to die, to bring me a large piece of fudge cake, frosted, buried in vanilla ice cream, and they might just as well smother it all in fudge sauce while they are at it.

Uncle Harry lived in a wooden house on the top of one of Worcester's hills. I remember only the kitchen because that's where we sat at a round wooden table. Harry loved round. He was round. The stuffed kishkeh was round, rolled into a snake on the table. And the huge challah and the Russian pumpernickel bread beside it were both round.

He hacked off chunks of the meat, pulled off pieces of the bread, and gave each of us some. My mother, my father, the three of us, his children, and last of all if there was any left, his sad, grey, overworked wife Sarah as bone thin as he was stuffed round. She liked her kitchen close, so she could reach all of it without walking and that's how it was. Zveetochnee tea finished the meal, brewed with leaves from the pirate's gold treasure chest on the table, served from a Russian samovar.

At the end of the meal, Harry, stuffed with food and pride, pulled out his money. "Look, Civia," he'd say, "my week's earnings." It was a roll of bills, captured in an elastic, and, depending on the week, it would be two to six inches thick, each bill wrapped around the next. I remember as a child thinking Uncle Harry must be very rich, finding out later from my defiant middle sister that he changed all his money into singles to make the pile bigger.

I never knew why our trips to Uncle Harry's stopped. My sister Blossom knew all the nuances, but we were never told. Then we visited Uncle Joe and Aunt Esther and Uncle Benny and Aunt Anne when they lived in Newton. After a while those trips stopped, too, although my mother kept up a lively telephone friendship with her sisters-in-law. What happened, Mother? Her disgust showed in her shoulder shrugs and pursed lips. She clearly didn't approve of her brothers or their divorces. Nobody was happier than my father who never liked his brothers-in-law in the first place.

The complexity of family relationships has always fascinated me. Greek tragedies are built on the themes of love and hate, loyalty and disloyalty, kindness and cruelty – all of the human interactions that flow through family ties. The classics continue to enthrall readers today because, as old as the stories are, the themes are still relevant. Plays, movies, and books mine rich plots from them. Newspapers scream their headlines. But to a little girl aching for family togetherness, I was sad that we didn't visit any more, even though I was afraid of Uncle Benny when he pulled me to him and rubbed my fat behind. I missed my cousins Sonny and Melvin. In adulthood I was sad that Sonny had been killed in World War II and that Joe's public display turned out to be a fraud. To welcome his sons home from the war he gave a party at which he presented each with a $1,000 check. But like everything else about my mother's brothers, it was fake. When the boys went to cash their checks there was no money in the bank. "What did you expect?" smiled my father.

Part One — Her Life

The wedding — July 25, 1918

As I mention in many of the stories I tell about my mother, she told me very little about her life in Russia. I know she was frightened and lonely. Her stepmothers were unkind, either giving her no attention or lashing out at her for reasons Civia couldn't understand. Abba and ElkaRisha, the oldest siblings, loved her and were caring, but she saw very little of them. Her other brothers and her sister Munya were rough and demanding, so she found her apprenticeship a blessing in its way. She worked hard, but she learned a lot and was surrounded by cousins and friends as she worked. When she returned to her home she met Meyer who was gentle and who adored her. Her new life began with her escape to America.

Civia is Born — July 25, 1898, Lepel, Russia

Barsha lay on the large feather mattress, laboring over the birth of her eighth child. The Moomah Sorah, the midwife who helped Barsha deliver all of her children, frowned.

--You are too old to be having more children, Barsha, she muttered under her breath. Your oldest child is twenty already. She is a grown woman who will soon have children of her own. You have five sons, all healthy, praise God, and two daughters, healthy as well. You have been blessed until now. Who knows what this one will be like? If she lives, muttered Sorah under her breath.

Barsha smiled at her friend as Sorah wiped the sweat from her face with a rough piece of cotton.

--Sorah, you will see. She will be muzinka, the baby, and she will be the best one of all. She will be like Abba and ElkaRisha, my two oldest, not like the others who are unkind and selfish. She will be smart and good. She will be called Civia after my great aunt and she will be healthy.

Barsha stopped talking as another pain pushed the breath from her body. Four hours later Sorah and Elka-Risha eased Civia out of Barsha's exhausted body, washed her with clean rags, cut the umbilical cord with dressmaker scissors they had heated in the wood stove, and laid the baby at Barsha's breast. Civia nuzzled as Barsha smiled. The mother began a Yiddish lullaby.

--Unter babele's vigele, shtait a visah tzigele . . .

Civia, too young to understand the words, but not too young to feel the love of her mother, nursed contentedly.

--*Under baby's crib there is a white onion. The onion will go searching for raisins and almonds. They are very sweet and my baby will grow to be healthy and fresh.*

Civia and Barsha slept.

Civia, 1898-1902

How do I imagine my mother's earliest years? I know her mother was an old woman at forty, worn out from delivering eight children, from washing clothes on a scrub board in an old tin tub, rubbing her hands raw with lye soap. Arthritis may have already set in, back aching as she wrung the clothes by hand and hung them on lines strung on wooden poles in the yard. Her back must have ached, too, when she was cooking and baking, pulling the heavy iron pans off the stove and out of the oven. When she fed the chickens and milked the cows before dawn, when she set the dough to rise before she saw the sun come up, when she swept up the dirt floor with a broom made from straw – all of her chores must have worn her down each day.

At night, when everyone was fed and quiet for the night, when she sat by the fire and did the mending and the darning of the clothing and socks for eight children and her husband, perhaps she rested then just before falling into bed herself. ElkaRisha helped her until she married and moved out to live with her husband, and Munya did whatever a ten-year-old could do, but the sons all worked in the tailor shop next door, which Chaim ruled with an iron hand. Maybe the boys brought in the wood for the fire and the water from the well. If they didn't, then Barsha carried the heavy wooden yoke on her shoulders, the buckets of water sloshing as she walked.

Ceil must have learned early on that when Chaim came home from his three daily trips to the Temple, Barsha's first job was to wait on him. She fed him thick slices of black bread, with butter if they had it, and kept the samovars filled with hot tea.

She brought him his tea in a tall glass, on a saucer filled with sugar cubes, and smiled at her husband as he held each cube in his teeth and slurped the tea through it until it melted. He smacked his lips when he finished and held up his hands for "Quiet" when he was through. When Chaim lay down on the feather bed all activity in the house stopped.

--Papa is sleeping, whispered Barsha. --Shah.

Even the rowdy boys tiptoed and stopped their fighting. Waking Papa was worth your life. He'd reach for the thick stick he kept next to the stove and beat them black and blue if they woke him from his nap. Rested, satisfied, re-freshed, Chaim would straighten his clothes and go back to the cleaning and dyeing shop next door. He smiled briefly at his sons who made sure they were laboring over huge vats of cleaning fluid or dye, or running hot irons over freshly dyed fabric. ElkaRisha would be working quietly in the corner of the shop where the light came in through a window, sewing buttons and torn seams on the garments that the neighbor women had just finished. Munya sat be-side her, watching, learning, handing her older sister pins and different colored threads. When she was old enough she would thread the needles before handing them to ElkaRisha.

When customers came to collect their newly dyed fabric or their finished clothes, only Chaim greeted them. He took their kopeks and rubles, slid them quickly into the money belt concealed under his long black coat, and clapped the customer on the back.

--Peace be with you. Shalom, friend, come back with more work. We do the best work you will find. We will never cheat you. My sons and daughters do only quality work. They are never lazy. Come back.

He beamed at the customer, turning back to his children with a scowl when the satisfied man left.

--And don't ever do anything they could complain about! You will regret it.

Then Chaim smiled to himself as he hid the money behind the bricks in the chimney. The pile was growing larger and Chaim was becoming a rich man.

At Home in the Pale of Settlement

The long, narrow room where Barsha and Civia slept was crowded. The seven other children slept here, the three youngest boys in one bed, the two oldest boys on the floor near the wood stove, the two girls in another bed, and Barsha and Chaim in the bed with the feather quilt in the corner. Now that Civia was born, the old wooden cradle was pushed next to the bed so Barsha could reach down and nurse the new baby during the night.

The wood stove filled the other corner, a woven basket piled high with split logs and wood chips beside it. Although it was warm this time of year, the stove was kept going to heat the water and cook the stew which the family would eat for supper. The faint smells of chicken and potatoes were overpowered by the heaviness of the red cabbage that made up most of the thick soup. Cabbage was cheap, potatoes were plentiful, but chicken was scarce, so Elka-Risha used two of the oldest hens to flavor the soup.

A large wooden cupboard next to the stove held the thick ceramic mugs they would use for soup and tea. The huge, round black bread, just pulled out of the oven by ElkaRisha, was cooling on the shelf. The smell of freshly baked bread brought the boys and Munya out of the workroom next door into the kitchen.

--When is dinner? yelled Harry, only sixteen but he's already bigger than his older brothers.

--Shah, quiet, said Abba. Mumutchka has just given birth. She needs her sleep.

He tried to push his brothers and sister back into the workroom, but they jostled each other through the narrow door, hitting and punching. Chaim shoved them back into the living area as he barged into the room, arms flailing, landing on everyone in his way.

--Where is my wife? Where is my new child?

Barsha stirred, the harsh familiar voice rousing her. She looked up at her husband.

--Chaim, here is your new child, Civia, named for my long dead aunt. She will be a beautiful child, dutiful and pleasant.

Chaim reached roughly for the sleeping baby. He peered down at her, black eyes glaring, long black beard covering his chest. Civia, awakened by the noise and the pungent smell of cleaning fluid, cried and coughed, some of the milk she had drunk spilling onto her dress. Chaim dropped her back into the crib and stood up.

--Bring her to me when she is awake and clean, he yelled. I am going back to work.

Barsha gathered her newborn to her breast and began to hum, "Unter babele's vigele . . ."

--Stop gawking and get back to work, Chaim yelled at his children. Customers will come and we won't be ready. They don't care about new babies. They just want their garments.

Barsha's Death, 1902

Four-year old Civia clutched her mother's hand. It was cold and Barsha was crying.

--Why do you cry, Mumutchka?" the little girl asked.

--My mother is dead, darling. We are burying her here and we won't see her any more. But we will remember her always.

Civia cried then, too, and her mother picked her up, cuddling the child to her large, soft breasts. The winds howled around them as they trudged through the snow from the small cemetery on the hill above the stone cottage. Barsha tried to wipe away her tears, but fresh ones flowed as soon as she dried her eyes. Civia didn't understand it all, but she knew that dying meant burying

someone who went away and didn't come back. And it was
so cold.

--But I have my mother, she thought, so everything is
all right.

Civia was the "muzinka," the youngest child of the
eight Elkind children. She was ten years younger than
her sister Manya, with Joe, Benny, Dave, and Harry in
between. The oldest were ElkaRisha, her other sister, and
Abba. Only Abba and ElkaRisha showed her any affection.
The others either bossed her around or ignored her. Fights
erupted as the boys fought over the last piece of bread or
over whose job it was to lift the heavy vats of dye. But
they never fought when the tall, black-bearded, black-eyed
man with the gruff voice yelled.

--Shah!

Father had the last word, frequently the only word.
Even wild-eyed Benny and crazy Joe obeyed Chaim when
he told them to be quiet.

Barsha's arms were Civia's safe place in the rough
family. She ran to her mother when she was frightened or
lonely. She climbed into her lap when she was tired or hungry. Barsha sang Russian and Yiddish lullabies to put her
baby to sleep in the big bed with the huge feather pillows.
When she remembered, Civia stayed close to the edge of
the bed so her large older sisters wouldn't crush her when
they came to bed. She hugged the mattress to keep from
falling onto the floor. But she was worried.

Barsha began coughing the day after the funeral. She
drank hot tea from the samovar, with ground up herbs from
her garden, but the cough didn't get better. It got louder
and louder and one day she spat up blood.

--Go get the doctor, Abba, said Chaim.

The doctor was three days' cart ride away, in Moscow,
and when Abba returned, Barsha lay dying in her bed,

shivering under the quilt. Civia tried to bring her mother
the warm quilt from her own bed but she wasn't big
enough to carry it. So she lay at her mother's feet
and cried.

--Mumutchka, please don't die. Please don't leave me.

Barsha strained to comfort her little one, but the pneumonia made it hard to breathe. She tried to talk, but could
not. She closed her eyes as Civia cried and cried. Now
Civia understood. You could be dead in bed inside a house
as well as in the cemetery on the hill. You could die and
never come back even if you were in your own bed. She
understood.

She would have to grow up without a mother.

Civia, 1902-1908

What happened to Civia in the years after her mother
died? Chaim growled that a carriage needs four wheels to
be complete and a man needs a wife to cook, clean house
for him and take care of the children. He went to Shul
every morning, noon, and night, including a prayer for his
dead wife in the eleven months of mourning. As he said the
Kaddish he swayed with the minyan of ten men, pounding
his chest rhythmically as he mumbled the Hebrew prayer
for the dead. The boys who were thirteen or older went
with him for the night prayer while the younger children
minded the store.

At the end of the year Chaim growled and married
Rivka, a widow without children, perhaps thinking that she
would be glad to take care of his. But she hated children,
and didn't like him much either, so they had a stormy ten
years before she died. Civia's only nurturing came from
ElkaRisha and the Moomah Sorah who loved Barsha and
felt sorry for the youngest child. Sorah often walked the
mile to Chaim's house to get Civia and then they would

walk together back to Sorah's orchard. Luscious red plums grew on her trees, and if Civia stretched as high as she could she would just reach the delicious fruit.

--Ess, mine kind. Eat as much as you want, my child. Fruit is good for you. Grow strong and healthy.

So Civia would stuff herself with the ripe, red fruit, soiling her dress, loving Sorah and her plums.

Dave, her older brother, was sometimes nice to her, patting her on the head absent-mindedly. Abba was always kind with a hug and a smile, and ElkaRisha was her mother. But the others – Joe, Benny, Harry, and Munya – yelled at her, called her spoiled, teased her, and frequently hit her when they were frustrated with each other. Abba would intervene and she would hide in his arms until her rough brothers and sister had to go back to work.

School was her escape. She eagerly walked the three miles to the one-room schoolhouse where the teacher taught the children Russian, reading, writing and arithmetic. Civia was quick and eager, always ready with an answer or a question. She could run fast and tell a joke, so she got away with being a Jew and with being smart.

Only at home was she unable to learn. Chaim hired a local man, a learned man who spent his life studying Torah and Talmud. Moshe came to the house twice a week to teach the boys the Hebrew they needed to pray in Shul. They had time off from work to sit around the wooden table and learn to daven. But the girls were not allowed to touch the books, or even to sit at the table. So Civia huddled in the corner, listening to every word, and seeking out Abba late at night to show him what she had been listening to. Civia envied her brothers their learning, but she wasn't sorry not to be at the table. It rang with Moshe's loud voice yelling when a boy made a mistake. And it rang with the cries of the boys when he brought his large wooden rod down on their hands.

--Look at the book! he yelled. You are not learning, you lazy boy. Learn!

So Civia spent her years from four to ten learning to read and write in Russian and picking up some Hebrew. She grew strong and athletic from playing and fighting with her brothers.

Ten years after her marriage to Chaim, Rivka died during a flu epidemic. Scrawny at best, she had no reserves to fight the disease and medicine was not available in that small shtetl. Once more Chaim spent the required year praying in Shul, but this time the boys didn't have to go because Rivka was not their mother. Civia barely missed her.

Life at home was not pleasant. After the year of shivah, Chaim married a tall, beautiful English woman who had come to visit a neighbor. He adored Gertrude and had a fur coat made for her because the Russian winters were so much colder than the English winters. He hugged her in front of the children. Civia, who had never seen her father hug anyone, was shocked. But, she reasoned, maybe because he's happy with her she will be nice to me. But Gertrude was nice only to Chaim. She yelled at everyone else, frequently lashing out to slap a face or twist an arm, and Civia became a quiet and unobtrusive sixteen-year-old, suppressing her natural zest for life.

What was life like for the Jews of the ghetto at that time? I have no personal stories to share, but we have history to learn from. The Jews were hated by their Gentile neighbors, even though they were all poor. The Gentiles who worked the land were taken advantage of by the landowners who worked them long hours and paid them very little. Taxes had to be collected, but landowners didn't want the bother or the trouble of hearing how poor a man was or that his wife needed medicine or that his children were hungry. So they hired Jews who could figure and write to be tax collectors. Now the serfs had more reasons to hate the Jews who took their money and their produce. It did no good for the Jewish tax collector to explain that the money went to the landowners.

--No, said the peasants, they keep it for themselves to buy their wives jewelry and fancy clothes.

Downtrodden and poor themselves, poorly educated, the peasants took out their frustration on the Jews, those strange people who looked different, talked a different language, ate different food, and spent so much time reading and going to their small Shul. There they drank the blood of Orthodox Russians and other Christians. They made sacrifices to a God who didn't even exist.

So the Jews lived with the hatred of their neighbors and with fewer rights than even the poorest serf. They could go to school for only a few years. They couldn't own land. They couldn't become officers in the Army and they couldn't become civilian administrators in their community. So they did whatever was available to them, becoming small shopkeepers, dairymen, tailors, cleaners and dyers, butchers, shoemakers, dressmakers, milliners, traveling peddlers, tinkers. Some became traveling Hebrew teachers for the small boys who had to learn Torah. Others became full-time students at the small Yeshiva where old learned men taught Yeshiva bochers who were going to be Bar Mitzvahed. Whatever kinds of service they could provide was what they did to try to feed their families and raise their children. And with very little they managed and their neighbors hated them more for their small successes.

In the world larger than the ghetto, the Russian government was going through political and sociological changes. Parties were in and parties were out. Revolutions took place for different philosophies. But there was one constant called anti-Semitism. When the peasantry got disturbed enough by poverty, poor food, and lack of opportunity, the government would decide,

--Let's give them something to vent their anger on instead of on us, and a decree would go out.

--Kill the Jews. Throw them out! Burn down their houses!

It would travel from Moscow to the small shtetls in the Pale of Settlement. Thus were pogroms born. The local constabulary or the Cossacks, the Red Army or the White Army would ride through the town burning Jewish homes, stealing whatever there was, raping the women, killing the men. The peasants were encouraged to take part, and many did, getting even with Jewish neighbors for real or imagined grievances. Then, when enough blood had been shed and enough damage done, things would quiet down and the remnants of Jewish shtetls would creep back to what was left of their homes to start over. So life went on.

Apprenticeship in the Shtetl, 1909-1917

--But, Papa, I want to go to school! I like school and I do well.

The tall man with the red-flecked black beard glared at his ten-year-old daughter. His black eyes pierced her face.

--You are old enough to learn a trade. You will become a dressmaker. Then you can make clothes for your children. You are finished with school.

Civia knew that it was no good to argue with her father. Chaim had the final word in the house. She could not look for support from her stepmother. There was no hope there.

Perhaps her oldest sister could help her. She was married, had children of her own, and loved her youngest sister. When ElkaRisha came to the house Chaim softened a bit, but ElkaRisha was away and there was no way to contact her,

Munya, the next oldest daughter, spoke.

--Of course you will learn to be a dressmaker. Papa is right. Women need to be able to make clothes for their children. How else will they get them?

Civia looked up at Munya. She was so ugly. No wonder she was not yet married. Who would want her? And she always agreed with everyone against Civia. Civia was sure she did it out of spite because she was the muzinka, the baby, and she was pretty. Munya hated the attention Civia got, and whenever she had the opportunity to make life hard for her baby sister, she took it.

--Of course you will become a dressmaker. Look at me. I can sew anything and people like the work I do.

Civia thought who cares? No one loves you no matter what kind of work you do. And, if I have to learn a trade, I want to be a milliner. Milliners make beautiful hats with ribbons and feathers. I could learn to make hats and decorate them. At least that would be fun. She decided to be bold.

--Papa, may I learn to be a milliner instead?

--You will do as you are told, Civia, or I will beat you with my stick. When I have finished, you will be lucky to be alive, never mind be a milliner. You start your apprenticeship tomorrow and the Moomah Gittel expects you at work at 7 a.m. It's a thirty-minute walk, so you have to get up very early to dress and eat before you go. Take some bread for lunch and we will see you back home in time for dinner. You work from 7:00 to 6:00. Next year you will be old enough to live there. And I expect to hear only good reports from Gittel. You will be working with six other girls.

Civia tried to stop the tears that were flowing, but the best she could do was to back out of the room and go to her mattress in the far corner of the house. She had the place farthest from the fire because she was the youngest. She buried herself under the scratchy blanket and cried. Tomorrow she would start her new life.

Meyer Comes to Work for Chaim, 1910

About my father's early years, I know so little. I do know he came from Mohliver, a town smaller than Lepel where my mother's family lived. I learned this when I heard their arguments about Russia.

"We had electricity," my father would say.

"You didn't even have oil lamps," my mother would answer. "You read by candlelight."

"We had plenty of food."

"You ate nothing but cabbage and potatoes," she would answer. And it went on.

Meyer's parents sent him to work for Chaim when he was twelve. They were poor, the Gorfinkels, and had no way to provide for a son that old. He was too old for school and old enough to use the skills of dyeing and pressing that his father had taught him. He could learn more while he worked.

They probably had heard of Chaim's business, a successful cleaning and dyeing operation, from the itinerant peddlers who traveled by horse-drawn wagons from city to city, bringing goods and news. Some of their trade was in rags, pieces cut from the sewing that Manya and ElkaRisha did, and a housewife might ask where this colorful fabric came from.

--From the shop of Chaim in Lepel, the peddler would answer.

--That's where Meyer will go to work, his mother decided.

The peddler gave Meyer the directions that would take

him eighty miles down river.

Meyer arrived at Chaim's home and shop the year after Civia was apprenticed to the dressmaker, so they didn't see much of each other because Civia lived at her workplace and Meyer lived with the Elkinds. But Civia came home for the High Holidays, Rosh Hashanah or Yom Kippur, the days when Jews did no work outside the home or even inside the home if they were truly Orthodox. She was maturing into a tall, broad, dark-eyed, sturdy woman with small, white teeth and a beautiful smile. She was full of the joy of being alive, and her work filled her with pride.

She was good at it, she knew, even if her teacher gave her very few compliments. She was happy, too, because she was living away from her abusive brothers and sharp-tongued sister Munya, and the stepmother who was jealous of her youth and beauty. At work she had the company of six other young girls, a few of them her cousins, and even though they were forbidden to talk to each other when they worked, they could smile during the day and whisper when they went to bed. Three slept in each of the feather beds, keeping each other warm and trading secrets as children do the world over. So it was an assured, happy young woman Meyer saw when Civia came home to visit.

Meyer was a slim, handsome, fair, blue-eyed boy, intelligent and curious about the world. He listened to the men when they talked in the shop, the older workers who would become his brothers-in-law and the customers who came to drop off or pick up clothes. He listened to the women who brought the finished garments they made of the fabrics Chaim's shop dyed, cleaned and pressed.

He learned everything he could about the country, the government, the pogroms, the opportunities and the problems. He learned to dye the fabrics in the huge tubs, stirring the dye over the hot coals, inhaling the fumes and coughing. He learned to remove them from the tubs, drop them into pots of cold water to rinse them, then drag them to the lines to dry in the sun. He learned how to press them on the huge boards, heating the heavy irons on the stove and rolling them over the fabrics until they were wrinkle-free and beautiful.

As the wet steam mixed with the pungent odor of cleaning fluid, Meyer coughed phlegm onto the floor. He didn't like the loud, vulgar talk of the older men – Dave, Harry, Joe and Benny – who told jokes about the whores in town and teased Meyer because he was a virgin. He was embarrassed by their talk and debilitated by this new, asthmatic breathing, his lack of strength, and having to ask for help in moving the heavy vats.

--Puny! Harry would shout.

--Fagele, taunted Joe, calling Meyer a small bird, a homosexual.

--Try harder, Dave added, kinder than his brothers.

--Why did our father hire you? asked Benny, the smart one who helped Chaim keep the books. We lose money on weaklings.

Meyer's only joy was when Civia came home or when Abba or ElkaRisha, both married now and living in small cottages nearby, came to visit. They reminded him of his family, his kind mother and sisters, all of whom adored Meyer. His father was stern, but he was not addicted to religion like Chaim, nor a hypocrite who went to Temple three times a day and then was cruel to his wife and children.

His father didn't love God and hate people. His father didn't believe in God, but he believed in the Ten Commandments and he treated people with kindness and courtesy. Meyer dreamed of the day he would marry Civia and take her away from her family.

Meyer's Travels, 1910

As soon as I saw her, I knew I loved her. I loved the way she looked – tall, strong, full-boned, wide-cheeked, dark brown eyes piercing everyone around her. Most of all I loved watching her walk, the way her boots clicked on the wooden floor, scooped up the dust, swirled up the dried grass. Her every move was filled with life. And her laugh – loud, even raucous, trilling from high to low and up again. Full and throaty, like her large breasts and her broad shoulders. She was only sixteen, but already a woman, and I was struck by her very being. She didn't know I was there, never mind that I loved her.

Six years earlier I had arrived from Mohliver, my small village eighty miles up the river, finding my way to this larger town. I pulled my small boat into shallow water each night, looking for help.

--Where is Ykaterina? I'd ask.

--It's near Kharkov.

Civia and Meyer in Russia

I would smile at the local fisherman, trying to make my Russian clear and perfect so I would get directions to help me. I hated to use Russian because I hated Russia, the Czar, the pogroms, the poverty, but I didn't dare talk Yiddish because then they'd throw rocks at me and give me bad directions on purpose. So I spoke Russian very carefully.

--Please sir, I need to go to Ykaterina Slavska Gubernya.

--It's near Kharkov, they'd say.

--I have a job there. The fisherman would smile at me, for I was a fine looking boy of 13, strong, tall, clean from bathing in the river, and polite. Just as I hoped, they thought I was a Gentile.

It took me two weeks to reach my destination, rowing all day and part of the night, but I found my way to the small village into the Pale of Settlement. It was safe now to talk Yiddish because only Jews lived here.

--Where does Chaim Elkind live? I asked a villager. He runs a cleaning and dyeing store. I'm a dyer and a presser. He has a job for me.

--Oh, really? He's rich. He's very religious. He's a mean one. Good luck.

I stowed my boat, covering it carefully with the heavy cloth I brought with me, burying it in the rocks, pulling it deep into the trees on the riverbed. I might need it if things didn't go well.

I was lucky to have a job to go to. A cousin of a cousin, a peddler, knew about the Elkind shop and told my mother. A friend had been there, knew that the old man needed a dyer, young and strong, able to move the heavy, wet fabrics in the cold of the Russian winter. Sometimes they froze into stiff boards, and hands stuck to them. It took youth and energy and hunger to drive a man to do this work and I had all of these. There was nothing for me at home in Mohliver, where my large family was starving because of too many mouths to feed.

--Go, my son, you're old enough to earn your own living. You can make your way in the world. Find Chaim Elkind and work for him. Please God maybe you will even find your way to America. My mother smiled at me as she wiped tears from her eyes.

My eyes, too, were bitter with tears when I left my mother, my four sisters and two brothers. I had been happy in my home, even though we were hungry. My father had given me the only gift he had to give; he had taught me a trade. I was a good dyer and a good presser. I could earn my way.

The Wedding, July 25, 1918

Meyer leaned against his bride as the Rabbi sang the words of the wedding service. In Hebrew he asked Civia if she took Meyer as her husband. Yes, she told him in Russian.

--Ret uff Ivrit! He scowled at her.

She didn't speak Hebrew well, so she couldn't do as he asked, but she told him yes in Yiddish.

--Besser, said the Rabbi.

Then he turned to Meyer who smiled at his bride as he told the Rabbi yes in Hebrew. The Rabbi turned to Elka-Risha, Civia's oldest sister, for her acknowledgment that all was right with this marriage. ElkaRisha was radiant. Her favorite sister, the baby in the family, was getting married and she liked Meyer. Abba, the oldest brother, nodded and smiled at the same time. He would go to Moomah Sorah's house with the bride and groom that night so he could show them what married people did in the marriage bed. The Rabbi sighed. All was well.

He knew these two young people had no one else to turn to. Civia's father Chaim was dead, the victim of a heart attack a year earlier when his house burned to the ground, taking with it all the gold he had hidden in the brick chimney. Her mother had been gone fifteen years, dying of pneumonia when Civia was four. The feather quilt that had covered her dead body was Civia's only inheritance. A poor dowry, but Meyer didn't care. He adored this woman who was now his wife.

There were no parents to attend the wedding. Meyer had lived in the small shack in back of the house while he was working and was by now a member of the household. But now the house, the business, the father, all were gone and the newlyweds had only each other and a room with the Moomah Sorah, the warm and wonderful woman who loved Civia and took them in.

The Rabbi sighed again. He was a small, old man who lived in the small Shul that was scarred with the pillages of the Ukrainian soldiers, the Czar's soldiers, and now the Bolshevik soldiers. It didn't matter who revolted, or who was in power, everyone hated the Jews and everyone came to steal, to rape, to destroy. The Shul had a few benches, a pair of brass candlesticks that the Rabbi had managed to hide, and Thanks-be-to-God, the sacred Torah scroll, old and cracked, but still theirs. He opened it now and read the weekly portion in careful, singsong Hebrew. Civia knew only a little Hebrew but Meyer was able to follow along as the Rabbi sang the text. He didn't know the meaning of the words, but he knew the words and the melody from his years of tutoring when he and his brothers were instructed at their kitchen table. He remembered the teacher hitting his knuckles with a ruler when he sang a note wrong. So he grimaced as he listened.

Civia felt his tenseness against her. She squeezed his

arm to reassure him, and he shifted his weight from his arthritic leg to his good one. Finally the Rabbi was finished. Meyer took out the thin, white gold band he had managed to buy with his few savings and slipped it onto her finger. We are married, he thought. We are married.

ElkaRisha and Abba hugged them and poured wine while they all sang the blessing. Civia knew these words from having heard her brothers sing them over the years. "Blessed art Thou, oh Lord our God, King of the universe, Creator of the fruit of the vine." Yes, she thought, the fruit of the vine. We will have this in our lives and we will have peace and safety. We will go to America. We will have the fruit of the vine and bread from the earth. We will have children and we will educate them. We will not be afraid. We will be free. Meyerke, my husband, we will go to America.

Meyer noticed her smile and was happy that she was happy. He had no idea what she was thinking or what was in store for him, but he knew that marriage to Civia was to be filled with the miracle of this woman together with her intense drive and relentless energy to reach any goal she chose for them.

Escape, 1919

Civia nursed her newborn baby, singing softly to her in Yiddish.

--Unter babele's vigele
--Shtait a viseh tzigele
--Der tzigel vert foren handlen
--Und bringen rosinkes mit mandlen . . .

The baby nursed hungrily, Civia rocking and singing. Would her child ever see her father, she wondered.

She screamed as the front door burst open, fearing yet another Bolshevik soldier looking to strip her and her food stores bare.

--Meyerke! How did you get here?

Meyer pulled Civia and the baby to him, holding them close against his wet, rough Army jacket, stamping his feet to warm them.

--I escaped, Lichtich. We heard about the Revolution and that the Czar and his whole family were killed by the Reds. They say the Reds are better to the Jews. They don't care about religion. They may let us alone and we can live in peace.

Civia sighed.

--No, my mun. The Czar is dead, yes, but the Bolsheviks are no better than the Cossaks or the Czar's Whites. The Bolsheviks hate the Jews as much as anyone else. They have been raping, stealing, and killing the women and children while the men were away in the Army. No, Meyerke, we will never be safe here. We must go to America.

Meyer frowned. He looked around at the one-room shack they lived in. He saw how thin and tired and worried Civia looked. But he knew more about the politics than she did and he felt they could be safe here and make a living, he as a dyer of clothes and Civia as a dressmaker. The Bolsheviks would need fabrics and sewing; they would leave them in peace. He tried to express all of this to his wife, but she just kept rocking and nursing, shaking her head.

Travel to America, 1918-1920

If I could be born again I'd choose 1919 so I could watch my mother and father as they made the decision to come to America. But I wasn't born until 1925, when they were already here, so we'll have to rely on my imagination. If I could be born again I'd also choose to be smart enough to ask them questions while I had the opportunity. But they are both gone now, Daddy at age fifty-eight and Mother at age seventy-five. It's not that I didn't have enough time. It's that I didn't have enough interest. The few questions I asked, I recall now, I really didn't listen hard to the answers, because of what relevance was life in Russia in 1918 when I was growing up in Massachusetts in the 1930's? As my friend Ira used to say, "Too soon old, too late smart."

So here I am in 2002, trying to recreate my mother's life, trying to imagine what she might have thought, what she might have said, how they might have argued about the decision, and how she might have felt. She had just given birth to her first child, in the same bed in which she was born, in Lepel, Russia, and the baby must have been crying as she heard raised voices and felt the anxiety in her mother's arms.

--Meyerke, Civia pleaded. We have to go. It's not safe here for Jews. Look what happened during the last Revolution. It doesn't matter that it's the Reds this time. They will be just as cruel as the Whites were a year ago. To all of them we are just dirty Jews. They'll kill us and the baby, take our poor things, and drink vodka to celebrate.

--Lichtich, Meyer smiled. I am not arguing with you. I know how dangerous it is here. If the soldiers find me they will shoot first and ask questions later. What they will do to you and the baby is even worse. But we have no passports, we have no money; we don't know how to get out of Russia. How will we manage?

--I don't know either. Shush, Mirele, shush. She opened her blouse to let her baby nurse, rocking as she talked. But we will find a way. My brothers sent money while you were away in the Army, fifty rubles that I have saved for the passage. We have to get to England, and then we have money to go to America.

Meyer sighed. --Oy, your brothers. Why would they send money? They are looking for you and me to come and be their slaves? They will work us to death paying them back for years, and when we say we have paid back they will say we owe more. They will never let us go.

--You may be right, my husband. But at least we will be alive. Here we will be dead and nothing will matter any more. They write that they are making a living, that there are schools for children, free schools, and it doesn't matter if you are Jewish. You can still go to school. Civia's eyes misted over as she looked at her child, and she held her closer. My mun, we must go to America so Mirele can go to school.

Meyer looked at his child and his wife. He knew that the Bolsheviks were more anti-religious than they were anti-Semitic and thought perhaps they could make it here, at home, without all the uncertainties of getting to America. On the other hand, he shivered when he thought of the Bolsheviks raping his wife and throwing his child against the wall. He thought again about the Army he had deserted, and he knew that the soldiers were looking for the deserters. Civia was right. They would have to find a way.

--Put whatever we can carry together, he said. I will go see the Rov to find out how we get papers.

Ellis Island, 1920

Land Ahoy!!

Celia and Meyer didn't understand the English, but the excitement was universal. People gathered up their few belongings, pulled their children to come along, roused sick ones from their corners and rushed for the upper decks where they could see the ship land after so many weeks at sea. The crush in steerage was dangerous as people shouldered their way to the fresh air.

People were being trampled, in danger of losing their children as they climbed over others and were shoved to the ground in return. Civia buried Mirele, her eighteen-month-old daughter, in her coat, grasped Meyer by the arm, and pushed her way through the crowd.

--Come, my Mun," she whispered to him, "we have to get to the upper deck." They made their way to the light, the soft whimper of the child audible only to them through the layers of clothing.

--The Statue of Liberty!!! a sailor yelled.

Meyer and Celia had no idea what it was, but, after eighteen months of overland and boat travel, there was the Lady beckoning to them and welcoming them to New York Harbor. The throngs of immigrants crowded the rail, laughing out loud and screaming to each other in Russian, in Polish, in German, in Dutch, in Czech, and in Yiddish. Tall buildings, fresh sea air, blue sky, this was the Promised Land. Celia tied Mirele into her coat, picked up their cardboard suitcase filled with baby clothes, and clutched her feather quilt under her other arm.

--Everything is fine, my Mun, she cautioned Meyer. No matter what they ask you, say it's fine. I heard that they send people back if they are sick or troubled. Smile a lot and just nod your head that everything is fine. Agree with them. They change your name? Let it be. They get ages wrong? Who cares? Just get through Ellis Island and my brother Hennech will be there to pick us up on the other side. We will be in America.

Meyer and Celia in America

America

Celia's Philosophy of Life

What made my mother so wonderful? It was lots of things, but the one that comes to mind most often is her philosophy of life. Her wild and wonderful ways, her upbeat nature, her natural optimism and her zest for life were infectious. Her analysis of a situation was just as sharp as her needle.

I smile when I quote her. I laugh at myself when I take clothes that need ironing to the cleaners or just plain give them away. And I laugh out loud when I see our children buy the biggest melons and cut them into huge pieces. Her threads embrace us still.

Settling in America

Exhausted but exhilarated, the young family settled in a one-bedroom apartment in Worcester, Massachusetts.

Mother was happy. Her child Mirele would grow up in
America; their future was assured. She would work for her
brothers and they would see to it. But Daddy knew better. He knew that all they wanted was their money back,
the fifty dollars they had sent for passage, and they would
get it from him no matter what the hardship to the family.
Feeling like an indentured servant, he was shamed into
turning back nearly all of his salary week after week while
Civia sewed long hours at home to supplement the
meager income.

She needed a loving family so badly and they had so
little. We reflected their loss. Daddy's family never left
Russia, and mother's family did nothing but fight with
each other. The brothers fought over the business, they
fought with their wives and children, they fought with my
father. He never fought back. He just withdrew. Finally,
when the debt was paid, he withdrew completely and we
moved to Jamaica Plain in Boston. I wonder how he convinced my mother. She was so much stronger than he was
and he loved her so much. She must have wanted to leave,
too, although family meant so much to her. Or the uncles
may have fired both my parents when they found out that
mother was doing some work for Harry at the same time
she was working for Joe and Benny. Since Harry was in a
different business and the brothers didn't talk to each other,
they probably considered this disloyal, and that may have
brought things to a head.

In Jamaica Plain Mother and Daddy moved into an
apartment in a three-story walk up, just across the street
from the store they opened. "Hyde Square Cleaners and
Dyers, Dressmaking and Alterations" read the two signs in
the windows that overlooked Center Street.

I'm told that a barbershop occupied the first floor of
our apartment building, another family lived on the second

floor, and my family had the top floor. It was bigger than Worcester and since there were now two children, they needed the space. I would be born two years later and we would then move to South Huntington Avenue to the second floor of a two-family house. We were ever so slowly coming up in the world. JP, it's called now, by the Yuppies of the Nineties who moved there and gentrified it. But then it was middle to lower middle class, a town of Irish Catholic working families whose fathers went to the bars after work and whose mothers stayed home to cook and clean for their families. Their social life as well as their spiritual life revolved around the Church, one block down from the store. The women were the churchgoers, finding solace there as they were uplifted from the drudgery of their meager lives. Women of thirty, already the mothers of half a dozen children, were old before they reached middle age.

I don't know why my parents picked Jamaica Plain. Perhaps it was all they could afford. I don't think my mother realized we would be the only Jewish family in the school and in the neighborhood. She, who understood everything about people, had no experience with American anti-Semitism, although she had more than her share of Russian pogroms and brutality toward Jews. But in America, the Golden Land, education was unlimited, open to all, and her children would be free to enjoy it. What she didn't know was that the school would be free, but we would pay for being different from the Irish Catholic children in Jamaica Plain. By the time I was born and going to school she had caught on. I never left home without my 'James Michael Curley for Mayor' button, which protected me from the boys who otherwise would torment me that I had killed Christ. As long as I was a supporter of their Irish Mayor, their Robin Hood who stole from the rich and found jobs and food for the poor, I was safe.

Funny – the cleaning store is a lot clearer in my
memory than the two-family home we then lived in. Only
the back porch, the driveway and the garage of the house
are clear. I can see the salamis that Kerry Arabian's family
used to stuff and hang on the back porch to dry out. Their
garlicky smells filled my nostrils and the house, especially
on hot summer days when the sun cooked them before
drying. The garage, the wonderful place where we did our
plays with chairs dragged from the house for our paying
audience, two cents per admission, was our fantasy world.
The doors were our curtain, the six-foot hollyhocks our
decorations. We hid in the garage while the audience as-
sembled, opening the doors when the play was about
to begin.

But the store I remember in every detail. Two large
glass windows guarded the center entrance door. The front
room had a large mirror and a square box for customers to
stand on while their clothes were being fitted. There was
a counter with a cash register where customers paid my
father when they picked up the finished work, and a door
leading to the back room where the work was done.

The men who came into the store called him the tailor
when they brought in their coats and three-piece suits to
let out or take in, to shorten or lengthen, all depending on
what had happened to their shapes since they bought the
serge or wool clothing that needed repairs. Daddy, a tape
measure around his neck and hugging his shoulders, a
piece of square white chalk in his hands, a pin cushion on
the box the customer stood on, and a yardstick to measure
by, chalked the clothes and smiled at the customers. The
door to the back room would be open a crack and there
stood my mother, the real tailor, watching carefully as she
watched daddy chalk. As soon as the customer left, she
pinned the garments where her highly trained eye told her

the pins should go.

"Why," I asked, "don't you go out front and chalk instead of watching from back here?"

"You don't understand, Babele," she'd smile. "Women can't be tailors; they can't touch men. I can work on women's clothes and be called a dressmaker, but not on the men's. Daddy is a presser and dyer, but he can't sew and I can tell by looking what needs to be done."

That's How it Was in the 1930's

In the back room was Ceil's machine, a black Singer she worked with one foot on the treadle, one hand on the wheel, and one hand on the fabric she pushed through the needle. Threads of every color and bobbins to match surrounded her, all ready for whatever came along. Beside her sat Mr. Feinstein, an old Jewish tailor, so shy he never spoke to customers and rarely to me. When he did speak it was with a heavy Russian Jewish accent to complain that his wife Rivka had given him a "nutting sanevich." At the height of the Depression Rivka had nothing else to give her husband for lunch, so every day he brought black bread and butter, his nothing sandwich. He used his needle to clean his teeth after his lunch, then to scratch his groin, then to sew. Then one day he didn't come to work.

"Where did he go, Mumutchka?"

No words came from my mother, only tears and sighs. Years later I learned that Mr. Feinstein hanged himself in his bedroom before the Depression could take away even his bread and butter.

Ceil was even more impressive with her handwork than she was with the machine. Her thimble on the third finger of her right hand, firm against the needle held in place by her thumb and second finger, plowed through hems. Elegant posture in her chair, black hair pulled back in a bun to reveal high cheekbones, sparkling black eyes, and shiny white small square teeth. One gold tooth gleamed from her open smile. She laughed when I admired her tooth, cuddling me against her warm breasts.

The fears, the pain, the worries about Mirele in the early years, all of these I can only guess. That they made it I know, and that my mother loved her adopted country with all her heart I heard over and over. The details of the trip and the hardships of the early years I know only vaguely. Whether Mother told me and I shut it out for lack of interest as young people whose world is only in the present do, or whether she herself shut it out of her life and didn't tell me, I don't remember. But she is gone all these years and I, not wise enough to hear it from her while I could, have had to make do with researching the lives and times of those years.

Time

Time can be a blessing, a gift, a curse, a drag, depending on where you are relative to it. If you are overextended and have no free minutes, not even time to eat properly, take a leisurely shower, read the morning paper; if you schedule your day moment by moment and can never let down for a minute, then you'll never catch up and time is your enemy.

If you're obsessed with being on time, using time, never killing time, it can be a hard taskmaster. Then time is a punishing, whipping overseer who lashes you, never rewards you. Like the Sears beltway that brought more work to my desk before I finished the stack before it, like the classic movie Modern Times, in which Charlie Chaplin was nearly killed by the pace in the production line; the more you use it, the more you are abused by it.

Yet my mother didn't seem to feel it. For her, time

was an opportunity. She worked steadily, at a rapid clip, all day and into the night. She worked day after day, year after year, millions and billions of stitches going through her machine and through her hands, and she never tired of working. She loved time. Her secret, I think, was that she managed time and didn't let it manage her. She did only those things that she needed to do in order to make the money her family needed.

She didn't cook; she didn't clean; she didn't do laundry. She hired people to do anything for her that she didn't want to do, or didn't want to take the time to do herself. Her daily underwear went into an unused sink, waiting for the cleaning man to come and wash it for her. If a week went by and he didn't show up, she threw it out, walked down to the local lingerie store and bought new. Time was more important than money and doing things like laundry was a waste of her time. "Time is too precious to waste."

My Three Bankbooks

"These are my three bankbooks," said Mrs. G., pointing to the pictures of her three daughters in their caps and gowns. She beamed at each picture in turn, then at all three together. "I did it," she said, "with a needle. I did it by hook or by crook."

I laughed with her, knowing what she would say to this new customer, for I had heard it many times before. Mrs. G, or Ceil "call me anything but don't call me late for breakfast" Gorfinkel, was THE dressmaker at Coolidge Corner in Brookline. Every well-to-do Brookline matron who wanted to look her best came to Mrs. G. because she was a dressmaker with "golden hands." They came because, like the best doctors in town, she was known as the best dressmaker, and if you wanted to be "in" you went to Mrs. G. And they came, too, because in addition to her dressmaking, she dispensed wise advice and counsel as she sewed. But this was 1968, when Ceil was talking with the new customer, and things had changed from 1934 when the story of Simmons begins.

"Simmons College was $300 a semester when my first daughter, Mirele, started. You ask, "What's $300?' but in those days it was like $3000 today. I didn't have it, with three children and a sick husband. But my children were going to go to college by hook or by crook, and it didn't matter if I had the money or not. I spoke to the comptroller because a customer said to go to him, but I didn't even know the word.

"He said Mirele couldn't come unless I paid for the semester ahead of time, so I said to myself that someone must tell the comptroller what to do. I told that secretary that I had to see that person and she told me that meant the President. She didn't think it was a good idea, but I did, and I just kept talking until she went in and asked him if he would see me.

"As long as I live, to my dying day, I will remember Dr. Bancroft Beatley. He was tall and handsome. He had a kind face and kind eyes. But most of all he had a voice that I fell in love with. He spoke English the way I wanted to, but never would, for he had generations of education behind him and I had six years of school in Russia and spoke English with an accent I hated. He used words that were beautiful, and he smiled at me as I told him that I had three girls to educate, I made my living with a needle, I had a sick husband, and I was sure that my girls would go to Simmons and graduate.

"He asked me how I would pay, and I told him I would pay a dollar at a time, but he would get every cent. I offered to do his wife's dressmaking free for life. I must have said the right things, even if I couldn't talk like he did, because he said that would do fine, and he made arrangements for me to pay as I could.

"After that I went to Simmons whenever President Beatley spoke, and each time I fell in love with his voice and language all over again. When my sick husband died and people asked me if I would marry again, I said only if it could be a man like Bancroft Beatley. I didn't find him yet. But I did send the three girls to Simmons, and I did pay every cent."

The customer smiled at Ceil and asked, "Did you spend every cent you had on educating your girls? Did you keep anything for yourself?"

My mother answered, "Tachrichim have no pockets."

I smiled, too. I had heard that many times. Shrouds don't have pockets. You can't take it with you.

I Know It's Perfect

I ran into the house, my report card clutched to my chest. My mother was working at her sewing machine as usual. She looked up to smile at me but never stopped the humming and whirring of the machine.

"What do you have, darling?"

"My first report card from high school."

"How wonderful. It's perfect."

"How do you know?" I laughed out loud because it really was good. I had worked hard and had done well, but perfect? "You have to look at it, Mamatchka, and sign it."

"Of course I'll sign it, but why do I have to look at it? I know it's perfect."

She signed it without looking, stopping the machine only long enough to give me a kiss and a hug. And there she was, back at work, the fabric flying through her fingers as she pushed it under the bouncing needle.

"By meer bist du shain." To me you're beautiful.

I Weed 'Em Out

Mrs. G. always had more customers than she could handle. They hated her prices, but they loved her work and her company. She's expensive, they would complain to each other, but she's worth it. There was pride in their voices that they were discerning enough to choose her and that she was discerning enough to select them as her customers.

It really was a selection process, for a new customer would come and would be given a chance by Ceil. If they measured up, they became fast friends. If they didn't, they got weeded out.

"I weed 'em out," she told me time and again as I sat with her while she worked at her machine. "Look at Mrs. Dillon."

I knew what she was talking about for I was there the day she did the weeding. Mrs. Dillon had just left, complaining bitterly about the price.

"A three hundred dollar dress and she wants a three dollar hem!" my mother grumbled. "OK, she's fussy about her clothes. That I accept. OK, she says I made it too tight when she gained five pounds between fittings. OK, she wants a new label because the Saks label from Filene's Basement isn't good enough. OK, I put in a Bergdorf label for free. Fine by me. All fine, but when she complains about the price, that's the end. She's a bitch! I weed 'em out."

"I heard you," shrieked Mrs. Dillon, returning for her gloves. "I heard you and I am gone. I'll go to Mrs. Green-berg down the street. She's cheaper, she's better, and she certainly knows how to treat her customers. You will never see me here again!" Mrs. Dillon picked up her gloves and flounced out the door, clicking her heels on the stairs as she went.

My mother laughed.

"Good," she said. "I don't have to listen to her complain about her husband any more. She doesn't do a lick of work, she redecorates her house every other year, she's nasty to her children, and she complains about my prices."

I knew from experience that you could demand everything and usually get it, but prices were a no-no. If you asked while being fitted how much it would be, Mrs. G. would tell you in Yiddish, "Du kenst nisht bavayzin a naar a halbeh arbet." The translation was not complimentary, suggesting that you can't show a fool half of a job, but the idea was clear. She couldn't tell you a price until she saw the work involved and every job was different. She was an artist with her needle and the work showed that. So if you asked prices or complained later, you were surely going to be weeded.

I laughed, too, but not quite as hard as my mother did, for Mrs. Dillon was the mother of two of our dearest friends and I wasn't sure how they would react to the story when they heard her side of it. The consolation was that they knew she was a bitch long before we did.

One Hand Washes Another

What on earth did she mean when she told us, "One hand washes another"?

How could you wash your hands with only one hand? But Mother said it so it must be true even if it was not so obvious. If I only had one hand it would be hard. I'd have to rub the soap against the sink, then rub my hand against the soap. I could do it, but how nice to have two hands.

When I grew beyond the literal stage, I understood. Of course it was true, I saw, that one hand washed another. And, figuratively, it was even more true. People were there for me when I least expected it. People stood by me when

I least deserved it. Love was coming from directions I never expected. But they recalled little things I had done for them, little things I had said when they needed support, and they remembered, even though I had forgotten.

Their hands were there for me.

Eat, My Children

My mother's dining room was saved for holiday dinners and parties. Otherwise we ate in the kitchen.

In her overworked world of dressmaking from early morning until late at night she created "take out" in our town. She got the butcher to prepare chickens, the produce man to save her the largest melons, oranges and apples, the bakery to make extra large breads, never sliced, so we could "break bread" together. Our world centered on the kitchen table with its red linoleum top and metal edge. Our world of food centered around that table, with FDR's Fireside Chats during those years, and without it when we lost him. But always food – plentiful, plain, huge – that we devoured at that table with the wooden chairs. We were four of us, my mother, my two sisters and myself. When Daddy was home, we were five. It was a happy place and we were never hungry, even during the Depression. I found out years later that my mother used to buy two kinds of food during the Depression – nutritious meals for us, her children, and cheaper foods for daddy and herself. We had to grow up healthy.

The dining room was special. A room away from the sewing room, sealed off by two sliding doors, it was a crowded, rectangular room filled corner to corner with an oblong wooden table surrounded by ten wooden chairs. This table had a cloth on it and there were matching napkins if we didn't go over ten. If we did, then the napkins that didn't match were discreetly placed at friendly plates.

The plates were matching Sears Roebuck originals, a few chipped. The butcher-prepared enormous turkey, stuffed, with gravy in a bowl, was the centerpiece. The challah beside it was glowing, braided, ready for tearing. Potatoes were heaped into serving bowls, white and sweet both, baked and hot. Salad filled the large yellow bowl from the multicolored set of Pyrex bowls that sat on top of the refrigerator the rest of the time. There was always "more in the kitchen" if the food on the table ran out. Frozen peas – overcooked but sweet – were passed. Two tubs of un-salted, whipped butter sat beside large saltshakers, ready to follow the bread. And the dessert – Bob Ware's best – the bear's claws my mother loved, cinnamon, raised dough pastries, the chocolate layer cake with white mountain ic-ing, and the huge flat sugar cookies with jelly thumbprints that stuck to your fingers and your teeth.

Laughter and the clatter of plates and silver echoed off the walls, bare except for the flowered curtain that covered the window leading out to the fire escape. It was a warm and wonderful room, which brings back warm and wonderful memories.

My mother didn't cook, but we were filled with love as she urged us to "Ess, meiner kinder."

The Singer

It didn't actually talk, not in words, but it did sing. It hummed, it growled, it coughed, it sputtered, it stuttered and it whirred. And when it was not performing, it listened.

When I was only as tall as the table that housed it, it sat in a corner of the back room of the cleaning store in Jamaica Plain. My mother sat behind it, pushing one garment af-ter another through its dancing needle, working the treadle with her foot. She stopped just long enough to kiss me and hug me when my sisters and I stopped to say goodbye on our way to school. She probably kissed them and hugged them, too, but I was aware only of her love for me.

"I love you, Babele, but now I have to make a living."

I was taller than the Singer by the time we moved to an apartment in Brookline and a store in Allston. Here the Singer was in front, and there my mother held court, seated at her throne. She looked the same, I think, but now there were glasses, which got in the way of our hugs and kisses. I didn't see as much of her then because my school was in Brookline and she left the house for the store long before we were up in the morning.

And then we moved again – this time to an apartment in Brookline which had room for the Singer and my mother's dressmaking and alterations business. The cleaning was sent out, so she needed only the front room for the racks of garments and the front window for her machine. Framed in sunshine as she sat behind her first love, she hummed along with the Singer as the fabrics flew through her fingers. She held court here with the same generous advice she had dispensed to her customers in Jamaica Plain, but these women were richer with different problems.

My sick father died, my two sisters married and moved out, and we were three – my mother, the Singer and I. I sat with her at the machine as she sometimes told me stories of life in Russia, gave me advice about living and loving and drank me in with her blazing eyes.

I, too, married, leaving mother with her trusted friend, now electrified, so she didn't have to work her feet as hard. But her days were just as long.

It was there when our phone rang at 3:00 in the morning, I heard my mother gasping, "Come, please. I can't catch my breath." She lived for a few months after that night, but never sewed again.

The Singer now sits quietly in the corner of my

A-frame in Maine, enjoying its retirement. If only it could talk.

Make Life Fun

We didn't have much fun in our lives when we were growing up in the Depression, but the times that were fun are not easily forgotten. Weekdays were routine with school, housework, homework and sometimes games in the backyard or on the street. But Saturday night and Sunday morning were something else.

Saturday night my mother would come home from the store, having finished her work for the week, and after a quick supper, we'd jump into the car for the weekly shopping trip to Blue Hill Avenue in Roxbury. My mother would rev up the motor and grind the gears in that wild and wonderful way she had, and we'd leave grey and dull Jamaica Plain to lurch off to Blue Hill Avenue, the crowded, noisy, Jewish shopping center of our world. Wall-to-wall traffic crowded the Avenue, as people jostled for parking and hollered to or at each other, either in friendship as they recognized a familiar face, or in anger as a stranger tried to muscle in on a parking space they were sure they had spotted first. Finally parked, we would follow my mother from store to store. This was not an easy thing to do, since she never walked, but ran from place to place, adding to her bundles in each store. When we did catch up, she would load each of us down with bags, give us a pat on the head, and hurry off to the next stop.

If I were lucky I'd get the bag from the deli, the smell of half-sour pickles making my mouth water as I sniffed. Or, if luckier still, the bag from the bakery, hot in my arms, filled with freshly baked bagels, challahs and wonder of wonders, cinnamon buns that could be pulled apart with your teeth if they were high enough in the bag. We'd follow mother as best we could, lugging the bundles, knowing we were far from done, for there was still the meat market, the fruit and vegetable stand, the special bakery where the CAKE was baked, and the corner newsstand for the *Sunday Herald*.

As wonderful as the chickens and roasts would be during the week, and as large and juicy as the huge fruits mother would pick out would be, nothing beat the excitement of the CAKE and the Sunday funnies, since these would be our Sunday breakfast. We'd drive home past the huge park where the Zoo was, and where people played baseball and flew kites 'til no light was left in the sky, and then we would leave noisy, fun-filled Roxbury behind to return to quiet, staid, Irish Jamaica Plain for another dull week. But there was still Sunday morning to look forward to, and we went to bed in a hurry, so it would come fast.

Sunday morning mother would arrive in our bedroom carrying a tray filled with three large dinner plates, three forks, three big towels, the CAKE, and the Sunday funnies. With her dressmaker eye and her butcher knife, she'd cut the cake, built to serve twelve, into three even pieces, hand us each our plate, divide up the Sunday funnies, and leave us to our pleasure. It's a good seventy-five years later, but I can still see, taste and smell that cake, nor have I seen one like it since.

Some magician who may have been a brick layer when not baking cakes, and some poet who understood children, must have engineered this cake together and decided to name it a Checkerboard cake. Built from alternating wedges of chocolate and vanilla cake, mortared with raspberry jam, and roof-topped with thick, fudge frosting, each bite melted in my mouth in a combination of flavors and textures that lasted bite after bite, and could be retrieved just by thinking about it later. Add to that the Sunday

Celia and Meyer in Atlantic City

funnies, the fact that we were eating a huge portion of cake for breakfast, and had two sisters to laugh with. I don't think there was ever a Sunday breakfast to equal it.

The Russian Tea Room

Just my mother and me. I couldn't believe it. We sat close together on the train, her arm around me, holding me to her soft, warm breasts. My head was drowned in them when she squeezed me, her gesture of abundant love. I'd gasp a little, looking for air, and she'd laugh and let go.

That laugh! Deep, extended, loud, almost embarrassing. But wonderful, especially when it was about me, for me, mine. She laughed a lot. Even when something was hard, she'd talk a little about it, smile, then laugh. We'll fix it, she'd say. Don't worry. But now the laugh was about pure fun. We were on vacation, for three whole days, just the two of us. One day on the train from Boston to New York. One day exploring New York and staying with the relatives, and one day back on the train, going home.

My mother was traveling to New York to see her cousin Fagie who was very sick. I knew little about it except that she was the daughter of my mother's favorite brother, Abba, the only brother who didn't leave Russia to come to America. Fagie was older than my mother by at least twenty years, but she was "too young to die," said my mother. I knew seeing Fagie had to be very important for Mother to leave work, something she did only on Sundays and the two important Jewish holy days, Rosh Hashanah and Yom Kippur. And it would have to be very serious for her to take me out of school.

I should have felt bad about Fagie, but I only felt good about me. A trip to New York, just the two of us, and a promised lunch at the Russian Tea Room. You wouldn't think lunch at a restaurant would mean so much to a ten-year-old, but there was magic in it for me. We didn't eat out much growing up because it cost too much, so we mostly ate my mother's invention, "takeout."

So lunch at a restaurant sounded grownup and elegant, but there was more: the Russian Tea Room. The name conjured up pictures of my Russian mother's youth. I could have a peek at a genuinely Russian room and Russian tea. I knew about Tsveetochneechai, the Russian tea that came in a metal treasure chest, from my Uncle Harry's house. I felt smug about that. You'll show me Russia, I thought, but I'm familiar with your tea. Filled with fantasy, I fell asleep.

Our first stop the next day was at the restaurant of my dreams. We were seated at a small, round table covered with a starched white cloth, crisp napkins to match, beautiful heavy, flowered china, and a goblet of ice water for each of us. Heavy gold-framed pictures hung on the walls beside floor to ceiling windows covered with red velvet drapes. Candles provided the only light in the room. I clutched the glass, afraid of dropping it and shaming my mother. She picked up the menu.

"Darling," she whispered, "put down the water. When

the waiter turns his back, we are leaving."

My heart pounded. What had I done wrong? But she smiled her reassuring smile, which told me not to worry. Everything would be all right. We walked out stiffly, my mother pulling me by the hand. I didn't take a full breath until we were back on the street.

She laughed. "Too expensive, Babele. We'll find an automat and you'll have fun putting the money into the wall. You choose something to eat, drop your money in, and like magic, the food comes out."

It was my American Tea Room, no glamour, but lots of light and food and fun, and my mother made it seem like it was the best choice of all.

My daughter Sue, when she was editing this book for me, reminded me that we had gone to a Horn and Hardart together when she was a teenager. We had also gone to a Russian Tea Room. No more Horn and Hardarts now, but perhaps we can still find a Russian Tea Room for the grandchildren.

Going Home

"Don't worry, Babele," she said. "Everything will be all right."

We were speeding along the highway in our 1940 Plymouth, heading north, going home. We had left my sick father in Miami Beach, and we were going back to Brookline, Massachusetts. I was so happy to be going home because Florida was too hot in those days before air conditioning, too lonely, and full of cockroaches in our tiny apartment. But I was worried, too. Where were we going to live?

"I couldn't make a living there. People don't get clothes fixed when they are hot and sticky. They go to the beach."

But where would we live, I wondered. I knew it would

be Brookline because my mother wanted me to go back to Brookline High School where I would get a good education and where my friends were.

I looked around at the back seat. Everything we owned was there – our clothes, a few dishes, a set of silverware, and of course her sewing machine, the Singer.

She smiled. "You see why we shouldn't worry? I'll make a living."

At home in Brookline, front to back, left to right: Miriam, Blossom, Celia, Evelyn, Ellie Arnold

A Master's Degree for Ceil — Harvard Yard, Cambridge MA, 1965

We clustered together in Harvard Yard, my husband, our children and my mother. I was breathless with excitement, anticipating the awarding of my Master's degree from the School of Education. After the Dean's presentation, the procession would form behind him as each school took its place in the long line.

I stood in my cap and gown with the red master's hood over my shoulder and beamed at my mother who worshipped education, considered it the most important part of anyone's life, and devoted her entire adult life to working eighteen-hour days to support the education of her three daughters. I had sat with her for hours as she worked at her sewing machine and talked about her aspirations for us.

A sick husband, unable to contribute to making the family living, didn't deter her. In fact, his objection to educating girls since they would only marry and have children, made her work even harder. She supported him in his illness but ignored his arguments and gathered her resources for our educations.

The comptroller at Simmons College didn't deter her when he said she would have to pay for the semester in full before she could send her firstborn there. She managed to convince the President she would pay by the week and do his wife's clothes free.

The long hours of work it took didn't deter her. She thrived on it.

So here I was in Harvard Yard the year I turned forty, giving my mother the diploma, just handed to me by the Dean of the Graduate School of Education.

"Mamutchka, this is for you," I said.

One generation from Siberia and we were sharing a Harvard diploma. Her look said it all.

Moving

Ceil pushed the fine woolen fabric under the dancing sewing machine needle faster, her foot pumping the treadle furiously. The louder he talked, the faster she worked. He was telling her she had to give up half her space and move to the smaller apartment across the hall.

"Just across the hall," he was saying, "not across the world."

Ceil took a deep breath to calm herself. What did he know about across the world? Had he carried a baby in his arms across the world? Had he buried a baby under a feather quilt so the Bolshevik soldiers ransacking the house wouldn't hear her cry?

What did he know about across the hall? Everything
would be backwards. Instead of going from left to right,
now everything would go from right to left. Her life would
be turned inside out. Instead of her sewing machine being
on the left as she walked into her sewing room, it would be
on the right. The iron would be in the wrong place and so
would the racks of women's clothing filling the room. And
when she went into the kitchen to make a cup of coffee,
she would be at the end of the apartment. Instead of a long
hall taking her to the extra bedrooms, there would be a wall
blocking her, shutting her inside another ghetto.

"Just carry your sewing machine across the hall," he
was saying. Had he seen the tall, redheaded soldier shoot
her sewing machine to pieces with his rifle? Had he seen
the soldier smash her cupboard when he saw that it held no
food for him?

--Jews are not allowed to have businesses, he had
shouted in Russian. --You have to go.

Ceil had muffled her screams into the quilt, lying on
top of the mattress, so he wouldn't hear Mirele crying
underneath her. She talked silently to God, praying that the
rough soldier would tire of his game and leave.

--Tierer Gott, she prayed, --Dear God, don't let him hurt
us. Let him destroy it all, but leave us alone.

She raised her eyes to Mr. Azavian, the manager, whom
she knew was trying to be kind.

"How much time do I have?" she asked.

"You have until Friday. That gives you three days to
move. And the rent will be the same."

He slammed the door behind him, making the racks
of clothes rattle. He really liked this strong woman who
had raised her daughters in this apartment and who did his
wife's clothes for nothing, but why did she give him such
a hard time? It was his job to move her so they could make

two apartments out of her one. It's what they did to all the apartments and he had left hers for last because he liked her. But she wasn't being cooperative and she was making him feel guilty. Too bad. It was his job or her feelings. No contest, he thought. And she had indicated she would move, so why even think about it any more.

Ceil straightened up from her machine. I'll manage, she told herself. It's just across the hall, not across the world. She looked up, "Gottenyu, My God, can you hear me? I need to give up my home. Help me do it with a smile."

Growing Old

My mother, who loved most things, hated growing old. She hated it in other people, and she hated it in herself. "We should be born old and grow young," she'd say. "That way we would have something to look forward to."

I watched her as she observed old people with their canes, their walkers and occasionally their wheelchairs. From her window overlooking Beacon Street we saw every stage of life, from babies to teens to the elderly. We saw weddings and funerals; we saw lovers hugging and having arguments; we saw the slow and the speedy. If they were her customers they would look up to the second floor window and wave to Ceil, working at her machine. She was as steady as the sunrise, sitting in the far right window, with the Dressmaking and Alterations sign, black letters on white glass, sturdy in the middle window. If you were on the streetcar, it was right above you. If you were walking, it was a bit more of a stretch, but there it was, reliable and constant.

The important signs in her Coolidge Corner block (Ceil called it Coolidge's Corner all her life, even when she knew it wasn't right, because people laughed and that was her pleasure) were: Ceil's dressmaking sign in the middle of the block, Bob Ware's Bakery downstairs, the china shop and St. Clair's ice cream and sandwich shop. The next block of stores housed a dress shop, a bank, a lingerie shop, the first health food store I ever saw, Simon's Shoe Store, and the crown of the block, the S.S. Pierce grocery store.

A word about S.S. Pierce. It filled the corner of Beacon and Harvard Streets, three stores wide on each side, a bastion of old New England manners and mores. Food was not on shelves to be handled and put into baskets; food was on display only. But at the long counter the shopper would sit on a high stool to be greeted by an S.S. Pierce shopping assistant, with a smile and a huge catalogue of groceries.

"Yes, Madame?"

"I would like some tuna fish, please."

"Of course, Madame. What brand? What size? In oil or water? White meat or not?" She flipped the pages of the catalogue as she spoke.

The purchase of a can or two of tuna fish could easily take ten minutes. When you paid for your purchase, you left the store feeling very cherished by S.S. Pierce. In Brookline the Pierce was pronounced Purse, after the old Yankee family for whom the store was named.

When S.S. Pierce went, buried by the new concept of supermarkets where goods were on shelves, customers pushed carriages, and checkout clerks rang up the orders, my mother said, "There goes Coolidge Corner. The Church, S.S. Pierce . . ."

If you were born old and died young, perhaps Coolidge Corner would have gone the same way, so that these pillars of our life would have been there in the 80's as they were in the 30's, 40's, 50's, 60's, and 70's. But, life and death go the other way, and we watched with sadness and longed for its energetic youth as it deteriorated.

As Coolidge Corner grew old, so did Ceil. She hung in there, tough and strong, working fourteen-hour days until she was seventy, when her health began to fray. It started with her move across the hall, where she really felt disoriented. Even though she coped and functioned, it was a strain for her to do everything in the opposite direction. She tried to feel cheerful and to present a cheerful face as she click-clacked down the sidewalks of Coolidge's Corner. The church was gone, her beautiful Episcopal Church with the towering spire right across the street at the pointed corner of Marion and Beacon Streets. The Church was built to fit the corner or the corner was built to fit the church, we didn't know which, but they fit like a hand in a glove. It was a magnificent brick edifice, elegant and serene, the site of entertainment from the window on Beacon Street, often from morning 'til night. Bridal parties in pastel colors, funeral parties in black, worshippers in Sunday finery, school children with book bags and roller skates, came and went all week.

Sundays were the best with no traffic on Beacon Street, fewer streetcars to block the view, and frequently a quiet day for Ceil. She rarely worked at her machine on Sundays, but she still sat there, in her window, to eat her meals and to talk with God. I don't remember a radio or a newspaper except Daddy's *Jewish Forward*, the *Sunday Boston Herald* and our listening to President Franklin D. Roosevelt's Fireside Chats.

If FDR were speaking, we all clustered around the kitchen table, our version of a fireside, and listened mesmerized. It didn't matter if I truly understood him or not; it was enough to watch my mother's enraptured face and her smiles and nods. She loved him as she loved President Bancroft Beatley of Simmons and for the same reasons. They both spoke English with beautiful Brahmin accents, they used long, beautifully enunciated words buried in glamorous syntax. She worshipped their talk and believed in their policies just because they talked that way. Perhaps I decided to become an English teacher while sitting around with FDR and my mother.

But, back to growing old.

All of these things were happening at Coolidge Corner while I was growing up, and my mother and I knew every niche and corner of her daily walk. We stopped to talk in every store, Mother introducing me as her "Babele" each time as if we had never been there before. But the tradespeople loved her so much they behaved as if it were a new introduction and so did I. We smiled at each other, realizing it gave her joy to say, "This is my Evie, my babele."

I was thirteen by the time we moved into the Beacon Street apartment, but that didn't make my mother think I was no longer her baby. I was, and would always be. Naturally I liked it better when I was in my forties and fifties, to be called her little baby when I was neither little nor a baby. By then it was perfect. When I was a teenager, I didn't like it as much, but it was always easy to go along with her since it gave her so much pleasure.

She was right, as little by little the elegant stores with household specialty items, designer clothing, fine shoes, lingerie, gave way to ethnic stores of all kinds, supermarkets, and diverse stores with less expensive merchandise and fewer services. The neighborhood was changing, too. Upper middle class whites were moving to Chestnut Hill or to Newton; Asians from many countries, Blacks from Boston, Europeans from Eastern and Western countries – all were settling in Brookline, famed for its good schools and services.

Ceil still had her cronies at Coolidge Corner, but it wasn't the same. She made new friends as she took her daily walk, but her old friends had gone with their shops and things were more rushed and less elegant. Still she soldiered on, shopping for her grandchildren, who had taken to spending weekends with her at Coolidge Corner. Her sleepovers with them were a replay of my years with her – the walks, the food, the introductions, the stories, and the fun of being together. When I interviewed each of them, they all told similar stories of Nana Ceil. They especially remembered their weekends with her and they never spoke of her being old. They seemed only to remember her being young, happy and bountiful.

Dying

It never seemed possible that my mother would die. She was too vital and too excited about living. And yet, age crept up on her and she, even with her strong will and excellent health, couldn't overcome the series of illnesses she experienced.

She got older, especially after the move. And then she got the shingles, a terrible case all over her head and her midriff. She "burned and burned," and there was nothing to help her. It lasted a long time, but she kept working, didn't complain, and kept up her cheerful talk with customers and with us. And then one night we got the call.

"Come, Albert. I can't breathe. I am very sick."

We jumped into clothes, fortunately living only a few minutes' drive from her house, and dashed up the stairs to find her breathing shallowly, then gasping, shaking. We called 911 and will never forget the young men who ran up the stairs with a stretcher, put an IV into her arm, and rushed her to the Beth Israel Hospital in Boston. I rode in the ambulance with her while Allie drove our car. She could barely speak. She had had a massive coronary and a stroke and we had no idea how serious the damage would be. I called my two sisters and we gathered around the bed in the ICU, watching Ceil with the tubes all over her body and the oxygen mask over her face.

Immediately we agreed that no heroic measures were to be taken. If there was anything mother would hate more than dying, it was living without functioning well. If there were brain damage we knew she would want none of it.

"No heroic measures," we told the doctors in the ER.

The doctors nodded knowingly while an orderly pushed the gurney away. No doubt they used heroic measures despite our request and she lived.

She didn't want to live, but she rallied enough to leave the hospital and go to my sister Mimi's house to recuperate. That didn't work out well because their personalities were so different, my mother not being a very compliant patient, so we suggested she come to us. We set her up in the dining room so she wouldn't have to navigate the stairs, and we managed for a few months. By then she was so ill that we felt we couldn't keep her safe at home and it was necessary to find a nursing home where her care would be more professional. We searched and we searched, standing on the curb and crying outside most of them, until we found one where the air smelled good and the people were kind.

My mother, despite her stroke, was well aware of where she was and whispered into my ear, "Babele, this is it." I knew she meant she wasn't going to live that way for long. Two weeks later she had a massive heart attack, was taken to the hospital where she pulled out all the tubes and died.

How often had she told us she would never be a burden and she would die with her boots on. My granddaughter Rebecca frequently thanks me for taking such good care of myself. That must be it, I think, my mother reminding me never to be a burden to my children. I'm trying.

Section Three

Remembering Ceil

Perhaps by now you know enough about Ceil's character and personality to understand why so many loved her so much. But I also want to show her to you, to try to re-create her bearing, her posture and her very being. Here are a few stories about her as well as some interviews: our son Bill and his grandmother when he was in elementary school, my interview with our daughter Susan, another with my niece and nephew, Carole and Bobby Chiller, an interview with Bill as a grownup, a memoir from my niece Phyllis and a two-day interview with my sister Miriam when she was living in a retirement community.

The Needle

I realize now that when I was six, the top of my head reaching just to the bottom of her ample breasts, she was thirty-three. But then, standing in the cleaning store beside her sewing machine, she was ageless. She was soft, she

was hard, she was strong, she was mellow and she smelled
wonderful. She smelled of raised dough cinnamon buns
and black coffee. Even today, when I smell cinnamon buns
I am transported back to the cleaning store in Hyde Square,
Jamaica Plain, Massachusetts.

The store itself smelled of clothing, and to my six-
year-old eye it was wall-to-wall dresses, blouses, skirts,
and an occasional man's suit. This was the place my mother went every day of the week except Sunday, the place
where she earned a living. When people asked her how
she earned a living, she would smile and answer, "With a
needle." It was warm standing next to my mother, not only
because she was hugging me, but because we were standing beside the pot-bellied stove which she had stuffed with
wood and lit at 5:00 that morning. Before leaving for the
store, she had prepared our breakfast, left our father sleeping in his arthritic position in bed, and left us with kisses
and admonishments about dressing warmly and being
on time for school. Inspired by her energy and effort, we
had jumped out of bed, eaten, dressed, and walked in the
ten degree cold to the store to say goodbye to our mother
before going to school.

So here I was, stuffed into my heavy jacket, gamely
trying to navigate in heavy winter boots, and wearing my
warm wool hat with the pompom on top. This was the only
piece of clothing that felt right. It fit and it was warm, and
the pompom was fun to play with. We all kissed Mother
goodbye and after she supervised our safe crossing of
Center Street, we took off in different directions for our
schools. I went to Wyman, the elementary school for kin-
dergarten through fifth grades. My middle sister Blossom
went down the street to Lowell, the middle school for
sixth through ninth graders. And my oldest sister Miriam
hopped the bus for the hour-long trip to Girls' Latin

School, where she had been sent because that was the way to go to college.

I was sure to be late if I didn't hurry, so I tried to run all the way to school. This was hard, first of all because I was so heavily dressed, secondly because I was personally heavy, and third because my legs and the rest of my body didn't work too well together when the circumstance called for running. But I tried, and made it just on time. What a joy it was to remove the jacket and the boots, and then, finally, the hat. As I slipped my fingers into the pompom, to give it one last reassuring touch, I discovered a needle sticking up in the yarn. It had to have attached itself to the pompom as I was being nestled into my mother's bosom, for that was where she put her needles when she was between sewing jobs at the store. She had pincushions in every size from small to large, but her bosom was her favorite place for needles until she was finished for the day. Here she kept the largest ones with the biggest eyes, and the smallest ones for the dainty jobs she also had to do. I panicked! Would my mother need this needle to earn her living before the school day was over? I couldn't ask my teacher, Miss Daley, because the first grade day was about to begin and it was not permitted to interrupt a class about something like a needle.

So I decided the best thing to do was hold it to make sure it wouldn't get lost. Since I am right-handed, and I would need my hand to do things in school all day, I removed the needle from the hat with my left thumb and forefinger and there I held it all day. I held it through classes in reading, I held it through recess, and I even held it while eating my sandwich during lunch. The long day finally ended. Clothed once again for the bitter cold, I took off for the store, and dutifully waited across the street until my mother spotted me so she could cross me to safety.

She gave me her usual warm smile combined with a crushing hug to her bosom, and I began to cry.

"What is the matter, Babele?" she asked, using the Yiddish diminutive for her youngest.

"I was afraid to lose your needle," I sobbed.

Uncomprehending, she looked at me with a frown. "I don't understand."

I handed her the needle, my left hand by now nearly frozen in place, unaccustomed pains shooting up my arm. Between gulps of air I told her how I found the needle, how I worried she would need it, and how I saved it for her. She beamed.

"Babele, I love you. You are my life."

She defined motherhood for me in many ways throughout her seventy-five years of life, but it was that moment, I am sure, that taught me what love looked like.

Re-creating Ceil

I can't re-create her for you as I would wish, but I will try. She's so hard to re-create because you'd have to see her, hear her, smell her and feel her touch to experience the length, depth and breadth of my mother.

You would have to see her when I was three and she was thirty. She was enormous, tall and broad with huge breasts that engulfed me, a pug of black hair pulled back tight from her high-cheekboned, radiant face. Her eyes were dark and sparkling, crinkling when she smiled; her teeth were tiny, white and even, and her skin was soft and white.

You would have to see her when I was forty-eight and she was seventy-five. She was dying; she looked small, frail and weak. I was now so much bigger than she that I cradled her in my arms, but she couldn't have felt as comfortable nestled in my small breasts as I had felt in her big ones. Only her teeth were the same, tiny and even.

You would have to hear her when she came to visit me at summer camp when I was five years old. She talked without punctuation, just as she wrote, and I thought she sounded funny. Never having been away from her before, it was the first time I realized she had an accent. Her voice was

Celia visiting me at summer camp

exciting and mellow. She filled her Yiddish with mixed metaphors, delighting us with her humor and the mispronunciations of the English words she sprinkled in.

"Why do I drive a Plymutt?" she'd ask. "Why don't I drive a Ford? What would have been wrong with an RCA? Why did I buy a Zenitt? What would a dressmaker do without her timble and treds?" She laughed at herself, and we laughed right along with her.

You would have to smell her. She loved freshly-baked coffee cake and coffee and used Pond's cream on her skin.

The combination of these wonderful smells combined with the scent of the only soap she used, Ivory, swirled around her as she reached out to hug me.

You would have to touch her. When she was dying, it was my turn to nurture her.

"Babele," she whispered, "it's noch ne'ilah. This is it."

The gates were closing on the Day of Atonement. It was all over.

Interview: Nana Ceil and Bill 1966

Bill was fourteen, in the eighth grade at the Driscoll School in Brookline.

Bill: I am interviewing a woman, my grandmother, who was born in Russia in 1898 and who left for the United States in 1918, arriving at Ellis Island in 1919.

Bill: What do you do for a living?

Ceil: I conduct a business where I live.

Bill: What form of government was there when you lived in Russia?

Ceil: The Czar's government.

B: A dictatorship?

C: Yes, the Czars ruled for 300 years. Then the Revolution broke out in 1916 and the Bolsheviks killed their entire family.

B: Was this government open – could a person talk about the government?

C: Never, he would be shot on the street.

B: No judge, no jury?

C: No nothing. No jury. The police had everything to say. A person would just be shot if they acted in a way the government didn't like.

B: What rights did a person have?

C: Very little.

B: There was no voting?

C: Indeed not.

B: How did the Czar get into office?

C: Well, 300 years ago, just like the Queen. The same idea.

B: What happened when one Czar died?

C: Then the next Romanoff took over, just inheritance. The son or the brother or the nephew took over.

B: How about economics? What facilities did you have?

C: Well, in the biggest cities like Kharkov, Ekateri-naslav, Bachmoot, in those cities, also Moscow, they had better facilities to live in. But in the smaller towns in White Russia they didn't have electricity, telephones. They had to carry the water in those buckets.

B: But the largest cities had these?

C: Yes. Oh, yes.

B: Cars?

C: No cars. I remember one day a car passed by. Maybe a Ford. The people started to run out of every little house, children, in the summer time, in the evening, they thought it was something from Heaven. And then it disappeared. We didn't see it any more.

B: Any subway?

C: Indeed not. In the city horse and buggy, in the country the train. With stations.

B: What was the average sum of money a person could earn?

C: Well, I'll tell you in a minute. My father had a cleaning and dyeing business and he employed fifteen men and each man got fifteen rubles a month with food. And that was a big pay then. I remember when I got through with my six years' apprenticeship I got twenty-four rubles a year and that amounted to fifty kopkes a week. A ruble is a dollar. A kopke is a penny.

B: How long did a person work?

C: As long as he wanted.

B: No, I mean how many hours?

C: Oh, they started about, oh heavens, about six, seven in the morning and finished about eight or nine at night. There was no such a thing as punching a clock. The people who were employed had to have a place to live where they worked; therefore my father had a little cottage in the back of the house where his help lived, don't you see?

B: Yes. What did the houses look like? Were they slums?

C: No, they were ordinary little houses in the small towns. But in the big cities they had four and five story houses and courts like over here with a lot of neighbors.

B: Were there a lot of families together with children?

C: Oh yes, a lot of children. Families had between six, eight, even eighteen children. We had a lot of children in Russia.

B: Education? Was there a primary school like here?

C: We had schools to grade seven but you had to pay, and we had a lot of children without education because not everybody could pay. It was costly, about sixty rubles a year to pay for a child's education. I was very fortunate because my father paid for me to go to school, but my older sisters were illiterate because at that time he didn't have so much money. You could go on to high school and then to universitet.

B: Is that university in Russia?

C: Yes.

B: In high school you had to pay, too?

C: Exactly. If you didn't pay you didn't go and that was that. If you didn't have money you didn't go.

B: There weren't many people in a classroom?

C: No, because it was costly. We went to school from eight to five for twelve months. No vacation like in here.

B: What were you taught?

C. Well, the girls had sewing and crocheting and knitting and then of course writing and spelling and arithmetic and we had a tschot, I don't know what they call it here, the Chinese people have it . . .

B: An abacus – you counted on it?

C: Yes, we counted on it.

B: And did you have English? I mean Russian? And on the social life. Was there a lot of violence? Like today in the United States there is teen violence against Vietnam and going into the Army.

C: Yes, we had Russian. No, they couldn't open their mouths with the Czar's government; they had no right to say anything but when the war broke out in 1914, Russia against Germany, and two years later in 1916, there was a Revolution and that was the time when the Czar and his whole family were shot down and that's when we had the Bolshevik government.

B: Were there robberies and murders?

C: Not as much because we never locked our houses. It was like one family altogether. There was no such a thing as knocking. If you came in and they ate, you took a chair and you sat down and ate, too. That's the kind of a life we had, like one family, I don't remember ever to feel that I wasn't happy. I was always happy.

B: What place did the father have in the family?

C: What place? Like the Czar in the government. You couldn't say one word. The father was Somebody. Everybody walked on their toes when he came in or when he slept. Whatever the father said was law.

B: How about the mother?

C: The mother they loved, but she couldn't say anything because those days she cooked, and washed, and ironed, and cleaned, and made things to sell. When she needed stockings for the children and you couldn't go out and buy anything so she had to make everything.

B: Were the families big?

C: Yes, it started with eight and it went to eighteen.

B: Were there opportunities outside the house?

C: In the big cities there were. In the small towns they never saw a movie or a train or anything.

B: You lived there for about twenty years so why did you leave?

C: Well, number one I had practically my whole family here in America, four brothers and a sister, and above all my husband, your grandfather, realized he didn't want to live there because he was afraid he would be drafted again. He was in the first World War, and therefore we wrote to my brothers and they sent us some money. It took us eighteen months to come because in every port we had to wait for some money to go on.

B: Did a lot of people leave?

C: That was the very last boat that went out from Russia. After that no one was able to leave Russia. We were very lucky.

B: Did a lot of people leave before you? Did a lot of people pack their bags and leave?

C: Well, before the War, in about 1914, you could just leave. But I was so young I don't remember who left, but in the recent years it was wartime for seven years and it was hard to get out.

B: Well thank you very much for this interview.

C: Thank you. It was a privilege to tell you what I remember. It's been a long time. I have been in this country for forty-five years. Thank you, darling.

A Picture of Ceil

To picture Ceil when I was going to high school you would have to place a Singer sewing machine at the large window overlooking Beacon Street in "Coolidge's Corner," Brookline, Massachusetts. There, sitting in the bright sunshine, she would be pushing fabrics through the flying needle, feet pedaling furiously, hands moving expertly. The seam completed, Ceil would pull the fabric to her face, and snip off the "treds" with her sharp, small, even white teeth. The one gold molar would just show as she pursed her lips to snip.

A broad woman with a strong Russian face, high cheekbones, black hair pulled back into a bun, she would be dressed in a fashionably cut dress, low at the neck. No

jewelry for Ceil, just a thin white gold wedding band,
the chasing worn through use. In spite of long years and
long hours at her machine, her neck and shoulders were
stretched tall and as straight as a ballerina.

When she rose to press the seam flat, you would see
well-muscled legs under a flaring hemline that came to the
knees. Her mid-high heels would click on the linoleum
floor, a fast walk. A quick press began with a spit of saliva
onto the iron to see if it was hot enough, an answering
sizzle, then a squeeze of the cloth sitting in the saucepan
on the ironing board, a flip of the cloth onto the fabric, the
hissing of the iron, an inspection of the seam, and a satisfied sigh as she hung the garment on the clothes rack and
pinned a ticket onto it.

Back at her machine she would urge another garment
through the flying needle, all the while listening for foot-
steps on the stairs leading up to her apartment. She knew
everyone's walk, and called their names out just before
they entered the door.

"Jeannie, sweet face. I love it when you come. Come
and sit by me. You never have to bring clothes to visit."

Jeannie Lerman, my mother-in-law, was a perfect friend
for Ceil. Jeannie thought she was an English Queen and
Ceil thought she was a Czarina. So they drank tea together,
which Ceil rustled up from her kitchen, and sometimes
shared a bear's paw, a cinnamon cake with fingers that Ceil
bought downstairs in Bob Ware's Bakery. Ceil didn't like
to eat when she worked because then she couldn't push
the fabrics through the machine. And Jeannie didn't like to
eat between meals because she watched her figure, so they
shared, instead of eating a whole one. But the joy of being
together and of sharing a cup of tea was their treat. They
really loved each other, and since Jeannie was my mother-
in-law, it was my treat as well. When they reported to me

about their visit, they said they talked about everything in
the world. I am sure they spent most of their time talking
about my husband and me, and perhaps we were everything in their world, or at least a big part of it. So Jeannie
became part of my mother's life at her machine, and Ceil
became part of Jeannie's life with her wisdom, her gift for
listening, and her joyful humor.

Surrounding Ceil in her sewing room, in addition to
her machine and her iron, was a long table on which sat
boxes of colored threads, perhaps a hundred spools. Boxes
also held her sewing needles and her bobbins, all of which
needed tender loving care. Ceil didn't have the personality
or the time to keep threads neatly wound, or to have bobbins ready in all colors, so she named my husband, Albert,
as her chief assistant. She called him on the phone.

"Allie, my bobbins and treds need you. You're a love."

My husband loved my mother, and was out the door on
his way to Ceil's to wind her threads and bobbins. While
he was there he would change her sewing machine bulb,
fix her iron cord, and take care of any odds and ends she
was saving for him. He responded every spring and fall
when she called him and said, "Allie, the clocks. Which
way do they go?" He loved her and she loved him
right back.

I See You

Mamatchka, I see you, even though you've been gone
these many years. I see you clearly, holding me when I'm a
little girl. I see your high cheekbones, your piercing brown
eyes, your slightly pointed chin, your black hair pulled
tightly into a low bun at the nape of your neck. I see your
flawless mouth, your white skin untouched by makeup,
your straight, small white teeth, and your radiant smile.

I see your straight back supporting your five-foot-five

inches of stocky frame. I see your magnificent carriage, a
Czarina in America, your strong hands with the thimble on
the third finger of the right hand.

I, a grown woman, see you, too, while you work at your
sewing machine. Your hair is graying now, your hands
have raised blue veins, but your face is still smooth, your
smile still wide. When you hear me coming up the flight of
stairs to your open door, you call out to me, "Babele!" and
I rush into your extended arms to be held.

And I see you white-faced and white-sheeted, tubes entering and exiting your body, your lips barely moving. Your
fingers flutter, reaching out to hold me, and I bend down
over your bed to hold you.

Interview with Susan

I remember my childhood weekends with Nana Ceil.
She took an hour to go one block from home to St. Claire's
to eat. My Nana Ceil spoke to everyone and said, "Here is
my granddaughter Susan. Imagine, she wants to spend a
weekend with me. What a love."

I always felt so special, so loved. She loved uncondi-
tionally, never was judgmental. She was a great talker, but
also a great listener. You could tell her anything and she
would understand. We'd go to Peek a Cheek (Pick a Chick)
for the biggest, roundest chicken to take home. Funny, I
do the same thing when I shop. I look for the biggest and
the roundest. I do it with melons, too. She taught me how
to pick a melon, how it should smell, how it should feel in
your hand, how it should weigh.

I loved it when I sat at her machine and threaded her
bobbins. You had to put the large roll of thread (her tred)
on the post, and the bobbin in its place, and then you had to
have the perfect combination of handwork and footwork on
the treadle to spin the bobbin and cover it with thread. Lots

of times I'd lose the big spool because I was going too fast.
So she would show me again; she did it so   perfectly, and
I'd try again. I finally got it and was pretty   good at it.

Then I'd sit on the floor with the big box of tapes, every
color imaginable. I'd hand roll each tape, dragging it out
of the pile which was a mixture of all the tapes thrown in
when she was working. It would take a long time just to
get the tapes out for rolling. She worked so fast that when
she pulled a piece of the tape to finish a hem she'd pull
too much, snip it off with her teeth and then just throw it
into the pile. Then I'd roll carefully, and when the tape was
finished, I'd put a common pin in to hold it. When I had
all the tapes done, I'd sort them by color. Nana Ceil never
cared about that, but I did, so she let me do it.

When it was time to eat I'd go into the kitchen to prepare lunch. I guess I was a young teen then, and she told
me to just fix whatever I liked for both of them. There was
always challah and there was always melon. Beyond that
you never knew. There might be chicken or maybe not.
But somehow there was enough to eat and there were the
thinnest paper plates you ever saw, hard to carry with food
on them, so I used to double them up. Then I'd bring lunch
into the sewing room, the front room overlooking Beacon
Street where the sun shone in almost all day, and we'd sit
at her machine and eat lunch together.

All of it was fun: the walking at Coolidge Corner,
the work in the sewing room, the lunch, the sleeping
over; it was always special and I loved it and I loved her.
There was a problem, though. She snored so loudly that I
couldn't sleep, and I'd just lie there hoping the night would
end and the sun would come up so the day could begin.
And then it didn't matter because we had so much fun.

She set such an example of joy, of hard work and of
family. Family was everything. I've always felt the same

way. It's always about family and now that I am married to Ian, it's all about his family, too.

Interview with Bill and Martha

Bill: Let's see. I remember going up there to 1382 Beacon Street, and sometimes my friends, Johnny O'Leary and Billy McCarthy, would go with me. She had two huge jars of candy. Crystal clear jars with all kinds of candy, mostly hard candies. I liked those strawberry things and I can't remember exactly what else. We'd go get candy and then she'd whoosh me over to her and give me a few bucks for my pocket and say take this money. She always had kind of a boisterous laugh and real warm laugh. I know on Saturdays she would hold court up there with all the ladies and she had a barbershop philosophical atmosphere. You know, the ladies would tell her about their issues at home and things and Nana Ceil would chime in some holistic quasi-remedies and everybody would listen.

It was a great place for the ladies to hang on a Saturday, but we'd kind of cruise in and cruise out. I used to go up there and cook steaks for her and she'd buy the biggest fruit she could buy, oranges that looked like grapefruits and Crenshaw melons, and sometimes I took her for a ride out to Ken's Steakhouse in Framingham. She loved the Ken's salad dressing and she loved the steaks and I drove her 1956 Savoy Coupe. It had hydra-glide transmission with push buttons and the great big fins, blue. I was about 17, had just got my license and it was a LONG haul on Route 9. It seemed like forever, that we'd never get there, but we did. All the traffic lights. It was fun.

I recall cruising Coolidge Corner with her, going to Pick a Chick (Peek a Cheek), the chicken place, and they all knew her as Mrs. G or Mrs. Jesus, and they'd yell Hi, Mrs. G, and we'd walk in to get the chicken and then we'd

go to Jack and Marion's, the restaurant there, and she'd
stop to do some chatting with everyone, introduce me, my
grandson Billie. But I think the thing I remember most that
certainly had an effect on me was her tremendous work
ethic. I want to die with my boots on. She always said that
and she almost did die with her boots on, working at her
machine. It was almost healthy for her, sitting quietly at
her machine, looking over Coolidge Corner, working at the
sewing machine.

The rumor that I had anyway was that she had a sliding scale of fees, but actually my aunt said she didn't. You
said yes it was true. I heard the Robin Hood story, that if
you could afford it without any problem you would pay
full price or more, and the folks who were having trouble
making ends meet, she would charge less or be free. We
used to talk about Russia and climbing trees and she said
she really had a great childhood. I always thought she went
to work for a milliner when she was six, but according to
Aunt Mimi it was a dressmaker and she was ten or eleven.

I think the most memorable feature of Nana Ceil was
when she walked you could tell she had a lot of pride and
felt very good about herself and who she was. I have heard
it said that it was a little sad that she did not get a full
education, but I never picked that up even though some
people might have. I picked up that she was very content
with who she was and what her job was and sending the
three girls to college and making that happen. I think she
just loved and lived The American Dream, you know coming over here and becoming a dressmaker and pressing the
clothes and delivering the clothes and assimilating into
the culture and a tremendous success story that way and
the generation after her with the college education became
even more successful as far as what we see as success. I
think her success was living through all of the hardships of

coming over here with a baby and a husband who wasn't well and making a go of it and feeling so proud of what she had, and she had kind of grown. I remember she had pretty substantial hands, a strong woman, firm, dark eyes, and a radiant smile.

She had such a strong work ethic. I think a lot of folks back there lived through some really tough times, some things we have no concept of and I'm fifty, I had no Depression, no coming over from another country with nothing, making ends meet, starting out at the bottom rung. I think that drive, that initiative, that ability to rebound after any kind of bad fortune and with a sick husband and not a lot of money and a young baby is remarkable. Also, she had a great sense of humor.

Martha: As the wife of twenty years, having heard stories about her all the time, the one thing that I see that she did with her grandchildren – Sue, Phyllis, Bill, Carole and Bobby. There is no question that she had the ability to make each of them feel so special. No matter how hard she worked, no matter what she did, her family came first and her grandchildren were just so important to her. There is a very warm place in Bill's heart, when he tells stories about her. He will never forget her because she really touched him and made him feel so special, a King.

Bill: She used to come to dinner at Somerset Road, and she'd park the big blue bird, the Savoy Coupe, across the street, and we'd be watching a cowboy and Indian movie and she'd come in and say, "Oy, I hate the shooting business."

And then I remember after dinner she'd come upstairs and sing Yiddish or Russian songs, and when I was little, she'd scratch my back.

Martha: Evelyn, with your grandchildren here, you

have a way of making them feel very special, too. The kids get so excited just as Lori's response was when she thought you might not make the graduation and all you had to hear was she wanted you and Boom! you were making the trip. You really wanted her to say come whereas some people might say, "Oh I hope they don't really want me there." I see in all my three children you make what they like to eat, you make the special mixtures they like to drink, and it seems to me that those were values that were passed down from your own mother.

Bill: I remember that. She loved fruit. I remember having to grab oranges with two hands when I was little because they were so big. And she used to say if I cook eggs they will be on the ceiling. She'd forget they were boiling and they'd pop. If she had one of her big melons in the house, she'd cut it into as many pieces as there were people in the room. So you could end up with a quarter of a melon. She was a great lady.

Interview with Bobby and Carole

When we were having breakfast together on June 8, 2002, in Natick MA, I asked Blossie's two children, Bobby Chiller and Carole Wacks, what they remembered about their Nana Ceil.

Bobby: I remember big fruit. I was maybe five or six years old. She used to go to the produce market on Beacon Street and buy big oranges as big as grapefruits. Then she'd go to Bob Ware's and buy the big sugar cookies with the little seeds in them and a circle of strawberries in the center. Maybe raspberries. Then I remember one Thanksgiving she had a roast prime rib, bone out. I remember food. I remember the roast, unsliced, on the dining room table in the big apartment.

The dining room was on the right side of the apartment with a door in and a door out on the same wall and a large dining room table, rectangle, dark wood. There might have been a window on one end of the room, a pretty good-sized dining room off the hallway with the sewing room on the left and a little couch. That was the only Thanksgiving we had there. I was a little kid. She looked like a guy, strong shoulders, big arms, didn't take any shit (laugh) and she carried herself like a guy, big, strong, tall, broad. I was a kid and you don't look at boobs.

Carole: I remember a lot of things actually. She used to come over to 11 Olde Field Road in Newton for dinner. I don't remember her when I was three and four and five, but I remember her small apartment, one bedroom. I remember going over there once a week. She always took me to Mrs. Reeser's for dinner. She used to go out to dinner every night because she detested cooking even though she loved eating.

Bobby: Oh, yeah, it used to be thirty-five cents, doilies, very Yankee.

Carole: She used to take me at twelve and thirteen to Country Clothes and to Mrs. Reeser's, very Goyish, very Gentile, creamed chicken on toast, and everybody was an old lady. Small portions. She also used to take me to Novak's on Beacon Street. She loved to eat and when she came to our house on Friday nights my mother used to make roast chicken, and to this day whenever I eat a chicken wing I think of my grandmother because she loved to eat and she devoured the wings. She ate it down to the bone, loved ice cream, and loved the giblets and the rear end. I try not to remember the rear end. She loved the poo-pek, which was the gizzard. She used to laugh like crazy, roar with laughter. When you, Ev, Mimi and my mother

were at the dinner table she was just hysterical. That was
the happiest she ever was, when her three daughters
were there.

She was attractive in a very different kind of a way;
she had white hair with a bluish pinkish tinge to it; she had
pearl white pearlized nail polish. She had great legs and
she couldn't wear flats because her calves were too big.
She spent a fortune on clothes and she would give them
away after she wore them a couple of times. Whoever
came in the door got them. She didn't like it any more. She
never washed a pair of stockings, she wore them once and
threw them away, she didn't like housework or cooking,
she never made a meal that I can remember except for the
Thanksgiving dinner Bobby mentioned. She had huge ear-
lobes and wore large earrings. She couldn't say "the," she
said "de" and she always said "tanks" for "thanks."

I have to tell you what she did. She took me to Magnolia Manor when I was fourteen years old. She took me to
Magnolia Manor in her 1955 blue Plymutt, two-toned, she
took me to Magnolia Manor and we stayed there for three
days and that's where I learned to do the tango and we
had dinner, lunch, walked, talked. She was very social and
she introduced me to everybody. The man who owned the
place had a wife who ran off with her son-in-law, I can't
remember exactly. It was the only trip she took me on. She
was very generous. She always gave you your birthday
years in money plus an extra dollar. I remember the sugar
cookies with the scalloped edges and the raspberry centers
with the seeds from the big bakery next door in Brookline
– Bob Ware's. She always used to come on Valentine's
Day with a big Valentine card; on Chanukah you got gelt
and she bought you anything you ever wanted. Everyone
who came to visit her would find her with the most perfect
posture at her sewing machine, working eighteen hours a

day, but always with time to visit. Always gave you money when you left, saying, "What can I give you?"

After she finished working for the afternoon she would take her walk at Coolidge Corner. She knew everybody and everything and was very, very strong, and once she had a fight in my house. My brother threw something at me in the living room, which just missed my eye. My father got bullshit at me and Nana stood up for my brother and my father stood up for me. He kicked her out of the house – Get the Hell out of my House, and Bobby was wrong, he almost killed me. A week later Nana came back and said, "No sonofabitch of a son-in-law is going to keep me away from my daughter!"

My father respected her because he admired her brains, her guts, and the fact that she came over here with no money and in a year she had her tailor shop and brought up her three girls. She could really be very tough. You had to be a very strong person to stand up to her. I think they really didn't like each other because they were a lot alike in a lot of ways. They were control freaks. Nana was very controlling. She was in control of her own life. When she put you guys through school she sat in the Dean's Office at Simmons until the Dean would listen to her that she would pay by the week. So her daughters could go to school. When she wanted something and it was important to her nothing stopped her or got in her way. If she had been born in America twenty or thirty years later she could have been a CEO of a corporation. She could have been a famous couturier.

Everything my mother ever bought she took to her to fix. Nana would fix the eyes, the hooks, remake things for me that were a little out of style, she would reshape them, re-design them. I remember standing in her room in front of the mirror, on a box, with her big yardstick and her chalk. She told me to stand still and not talk.

Ev: Do you remember she used to say put your finger in your mouth when she cut something on you? It was an old superstition about not cutting up your brains.

Carole: I remember her timble, her sitting at the sewing machine. Mostly I remember her accent. I have the tape you gave me. She went to Bill's school when he was an eighth grader. She told her story about leaving Russia and getting here in 1920.

Your father died in 1953 and I was only seven so I don't remember him much. He wasn't around much either when I was a little girl. He was a sick man in Arizona. I always got the feeling that she ran the show. I do say I have never seen anyone love their children any more than Nana Ceil did. And she was also very close to the boys, Billy and Bobby. She had a special place in her heart for the boys. She had no sons.

Bobby: She used to take one kid a week overnight. Carole doesn't remember going over there overnight, but I remember. It used to take half an hour to get down the block. She stopped and introduced you to everybody. And then when we'd walk away she'd say he's got an accent. She hated accents, mostly her own. One of her favorite words was Darling! She used to call everyone Darling. She called herself Mrs. G or Mrs. Jesus. She loved everything big, tall people, big restaurants, big fruit, lovely clothes, she didn't like short people, sick old men with the prostrate. She had a guy who liked her. Why didn't she marry him?

Ev: She said she'd never marry anyone. He'd be "prostrate with two bottles" and I think she loved her independence, not having to answer to a man or anyone. I had one man, one God, one family, she said.

Carole: I think when she was my age in her fifties she loved her sense of freedom. Her girls were grown and married. She could enjoy life. Meyer was fifty-six and she was fifty-five, very independent. Loved to do what she pleased. She'd spend money, never balanced a checkbook. Whatever the bank said she had was what she said she had. My mother used to say what about the checks you wrote since that statement? And my grandmother used to say who cares? She was a terrible housekeeper. Didn't like the details. She focused exclusively on work and her family. She paid for anything she didn't want to do herself. When she played poker and everyone said a nickel she'd say dime! She was a gambler. I wonder if that's why I love cards so much. She used to drink Scotch on the rocks. She'd come to our house once a week for dinner and have Scotch on the rocks. Only one drink. I was twenty-seven in 1974 when she died and I moved to California when I was twenty-one so after twenty-one I didn't see her very often until she got sick. The last time I really saw her was in '72.

She was square, square shoulders, big arms; my mother was built like her. But she was a size 14, she had great legs, beautiful legs actually, lovely hands. I used to sit on the back of the couch and brush her hair when I was nineteen. She got her nails done every week. She was a handsome woman. She loved having her hair brushed.

Ev: She loved having a massage, having her legs creamed, her hair brushed, a facial. I used to do that on the couch every Sunday when she wasn't working.

Bobby: Can I get a word in edgewise? Nothing has changed. I remember her driving like a truck driver. She was a terrible driver and she was afraid of the police. The Plymutt had a huge steering wheel and no power steering and I remember she used to complain when she had to take a turn. I remember how big her arms were when she made the turn, complaining. I guess because she came from Russia she didn't like authority. I wonder where I got that from? She must have told me that or my mother told me that. She told me if I went to Harvard she'd give me her car. Nobody went to Harvard, but Billy got her car. He was always the favorite. She loved me, too, but Billy was her favorite. She liked Billy more than me, but it didn't bother me.

Memoir of my Nana Ceil by Phyllis

What I remember most about my nana is feeling loved and adored. My every move and very existence were cherished. I was the awkward and difficult age of thirteen. I was not a happy girl. I had just bought a dress and brought it to my nana's for approval and possible alteration. I don't remember much about that dress except it was not a good choice and had to be returned. But even so, my nana stroked the fabric and told my mother, "Like butter, Mirele, like butter!" I felt brilliant for having selected such a marvelous fabric – and not at all bad about returning the dress – such was the magic of my Nana Ceil.

Mrs. Reeser's restaurant. A small restaurant in a basement apartment on Beacon Street. Cooking by an actual Mrs. Reeser, as I recall a widowed woman making ends meet with her home cooking. Sixty years ago when it didn't cost hundreds of thousands and hundreds of permits to open a restaurant. Nana Ceil would take me there for dinner. I always got chicken potpie. And for dessert ice cream. I remember being disappointed they only had vanilla. I didn't like vanilla but they brought it to me anyway. And was I surprised! Everything at Mrs. Reesers's was home cooking – and so was the ice cream. I'd never had hand-churned ice cream before and to this day it is the best ice cream I've ever had – and I know my ice cream!

But the special thing about Mrs. Reeser's was how every time we walked in my nana presented me to the patrons and to Mrs. Reeser herself. "This is my grand-daughter Phyllis!" as if she were introducing the queen!

SS Pierce's counter. My nana would meet her friends there for coffee. They seemed ancient to me. They must have been in their fifties, younger than I am now, but they seemed very, very old. They sat at the counter and drank their coffee black. It was served with tiny glass bottles of cream, real cream, back before everything was pasteurized. And they delighted in giving me the tiny bottles and watching me drink that delicious cream.

All I was doing was drinking cream – but the way my nana told her friends about how I liked that cream and the tiny bottles – well, she made me feel like the cleverest and dearest child ever! It was a magic she had.

The "materials box." Nana Ceil was a dressmaker. All the leftover fabrics from hems and alterations were placed in a box by the treadle sewing machine. As a child I would play with them for hours. I loved the feel of the fabrics as I ran my hands over the various textures – nubby wools, smooth satins.

Nana had affluent clients who shopped at high-end stores and fabrics themselves were of a higher quality in those days – so these were some pretty fabulous fabrics. I would luxuriate in them for hours. And, once again, my nana made me feel like the cleverest, specialest girl in the world for doing so. She would comment on my delight to anyone who came by – her helper, a woman named Zyl-pha, her clients, and to my mother. I felt as if she were telling them all how special and wonderful I was – not just any girl would luxuriate so in a box of fabric!

I would sleep over at my nana's house and she made

me feel like an honored guest. She would take me to Howard Johnson's for dinner and buy me toys and clothes and the whole visit was magical. But not because of the restaurants or the things she would buy me, but because of the way she made me feel. Special, cherished, adored.

As I got older things became more complicated. I was not a happy teenager. Things were difficult between my mother and me.

My dad died when I was in high school and I didn't know how to handle it. My Nana Ceil loved her daughter, my mother, and wanted to protect her. My nana was caught in the middle between my mother and me. She asked me not to make my mother unhappy, but I didn't know how to do that and still be true to myself. So distance developed between us. I so wish that I had had the wisdom and maturity to handle it better.

My nana came to my Cornell graduation. She was no longer healthy. It was a difficult trip. But I know she was incredibly proud that I was graduating from a top university. Nana Ceil's health declined and she died soon after. But her legacy lives on.

I remembered how my Nana Ceil made me feel like a cherished, special, and adored child. It was the most unconditional love I ever experienced. It was very, very important in my life.

So, when I had children I moved back to Boston so my children could be near their grandmother. And it worked.

My children, Garreth, Kyla and Zach, had their Nana who made them feel special and cherished and adored.

Interview with Miriam
July 2001, at her Retirement Home

When I interviewed my older sister Miriam I asked her if she had any stories Mother had told her about Europe

*and about the years before I was born. She worked with
Mother, doing alterations for her for several years, and
they had lots of opportunity to talk. Mimi and I talked for
several hours a day over three days. I am so grateful I did
it then because she died two years later.*

Miriam: I was born in Lepel, Russia, July 28, 1919, in
the same bed and was delivered by the same midwife as
Mother. Our father was hiding under the bed. He had been
in the Russian army during the Russian Revolution; when
he was wounded and sent home, he deserted. Mother said
that every week or two a different army came into their
village in White Russia. They gathered up as many of the
young Jewish boys and men as they could find, lined them
up, and shot them. The White Russian army, the Red Russian army, the German army, the Ukrainian army all took
turns, but mother said the soldiers in the Ukrainian army,
especially, were beasts.

We were traveling to America under very difficult circumstances during the Russian Revolution so it took us a
year and a half to get here. My mother's brothers in Massachusetts had sent Mother and Dad two tickets to come
here, but in order to come we also needed visas to cross
the borders, and that's why it took so long. I know that we
lived in Germany for quite a while and that was challeng-
ing because they had no money. Somehow or other they
found Jewish people who helped them. The women used to
cook taibele, pigeons, which were like white chicken meat.
I have a feeling Mother did alterations and Daddy pressed.
Between the two of them they found a way to survive in
Germany, have a roof over their heads and feed the
three of us.

After we crossed the German border and finally got to
England, we embarked from Southampton on what was
then called the Cunard Line. We should have finally been

safe, but I got a cold. My father told my mother not to take me to the ship's doctor until we had been out at sea for twenty-four hours, but my mother was very excitable and worried since I was her first baby, so she took me anyway. As Daddy feared, the ship's doctor ordered the ship to be turned around and we went back to Southampton. Apparently the doctor thought it might be something that would affect all the people on board, especially in steerage where we were. They put my mother in a home for aged women, they put my father in a home for insane men, and they put me in the hospital. But still they managed to visit every day. It turned out to be just a bad cold, but of course we had to wait for another ship. We landed on Ellis Island on January 1, 1921, when I was about seventeen months old. My Uncle Harry met us there and drove us to Worcester. Years later you, Blossom and I put up three plaques on the wall at Ellis Island, one for each of us.

At the age of thirteen when it was time for him to go to work, Father came from Mohliver Gubernya, ninety miles away from Lepel, a long trip in those days, to work for Mother's father, Chaim, in his cottage industry. He lived there and learned how to dye clothes. Because there were no ready-to-wear clothes at that time the peasants grew flax and linen, wove it and brought it to Chaim for dyeing. Then they took the cloth home, cut it and sewed it into clothing. Daddy found working with the heavy, wet fabrics in the cold winter very debilitating, but he also found Civia. They were married July 25, 1918.

I remember Mother used to say her name was Tzatzilya Yefimivna Elkind, Kharkovskai Ulitseh, Yekatarinaslavska Gubernya, and Lepel must have been the village. It wasn't really a ghetto, although all the Jews lived there together because they weren't allowed to live in Moscow or any large city. When Mother used to go to Charkov to buy dye for my grandfather she had to use the maid's papers. I assume she went by train or possibly by wagon and horse.

The one thing that my mother never got over was her mother's death when Civia was four years old. She was always asking herself (sometimes she would say it out loud), am I being a good enough mother? Am I being the kind of mother I should be? She didn't have a role model, just unkind stepmothers.

I can't tell you much about Daddy's family because none of them came to this country, but Mother was the youngest of eight children. Her father went to temple every morning, returning home for a little schnapps. He believed that his temple attendance was a sign of piety, of being a moral and ethical man, but he was pretty much of a stinker. He was tough. He despaired when the gold that he had saved in the chimney melted away during a fire, and he died a week later. I was named after him. He was Chaim and I was Chaya. But since he was still alive, in the Jewish tradition they couldn't call me Chaya, so in Yiddish I was Chaya Mireh and in English I was Miriam Irene. Miriam was a neighbor who loved my mother and called her "her child," so mother gave me that name.

My earliest memory of Worcester is when Blossom was born at St. Vincent's Hospital when I was two. Mother said it was time to move. We moved for several reasons. One was she didn't think Worcester was a large enough city for Jewish girls to be raised in. In addition, my father worked for his brothers-in-law, Joe and Benny, whom he hated. Already suffering from asthma and arthritis, he was cold working outside even with his boots on. We moved to Roxbury where Uncle Dave had a shop where they could work. Daddy felt like he was going to jail every day because Dave used to stand there and yell "Chak Chak," work harder, and Daddy couldn't stand him. My uncles were not nice men.

Another thing was that mother was doing the tailoring for the Metropolitan Dye House for Dave while she was doing tailoring for Harry at the same time. When Dave found out she was working for Harry he got very angry. Now these are brothers and they could have had the cleaning business tied up in Worcester among them. But they had price wars!! They were crazy.

They came to the U.S. to avoid the draft in Russia and Benny, particularly, was brilliant. He went to school but never studied; a week before exams he would hibernate, learn the whole thing, and pass with flying colors. He was basically an engineer, understood artesian wells and was very capable. Mother was also very smart. She had very little education but she was literate. She could understand and speak Polish and Russian; she knew no Yiddish in Russia but learned it here from her friends and became very proficient in Yiddish and English. A year after we moved to Roxbury you were born at St. Elizabeth's Hospital. I remember seeing Mother walking across a snowy field carrying you in her arms to bring you home.

I remember Auntie Munya checking my underwear to see if it was clean in case of an accident on the road. When we went to camp Munya said the "baren will eat them up." Mother wasn't worried about the bears eating us up at camp and sent us anyway. One day my father told me, although mother never mentioned it, that Munya said it was a shanda to have more than two children and she insisted that Ceil have an abortion. It was a boy. With that, my father threw Munya out of the house. He never let her in the house again.

I asked Mimi where did she think Mother's gootskeit came from. Her brothers and Munya were so bad and she was so good.

Miriam: Well, people are born certain ways, even with no role model. She was a very smart lady with a great sense of humor. Over these years of working with her in the sewing room I watched the way she handled her customers. Her people skills were so terrific. When she was sick in the hospital we ended up with brown paper bags full of notes from her customers and friends. People of all ages loved her. I don't know if I should talk about Irving. *(I assured her I wouldn't use the real name so she continued.)*

Miriam: Irving was a friend from Mohliver. He was almost family, as he had a sister or brother who was married to my father's sister or brother. He had to leave Russia because he was stealing horses. He was a piano salesman who used to come to our house to visit, have a schnapps, eat a piece of herring, eat a piece of bread with salt, and if he had sold a piano he'd have another schnapps. He had a wife and children and he also had a mistress.

He celebrated two twenty-fifth anniversaries, one with his wife and the other with his mistress. His daughter said that when she grew up she was going to get a gun and she was going to shoot her father. But his wife adored him, called him 'My Irving,' and had two wonderful children with him. I remember Mother throwing him down the stairs once. They were right in front of an open stairway and when he started to grope her she gave him a shove and he went toppling down the stairs. I saw it. He came back again. Very chutzpadik. He did a good job as president of the Mohliver Cemetery. The Mohliver organization is pretty well set for money. Those of us who pay three dollars a year for dues don't have to pay for the banquet; that's how well set they are.

Although Mum wanted to be a milliner, she was trained to be a dressmaker because then she could make clothes for her children. There were six girls who lived in the tailor's house. She must have been ten or eleven and she also had to take care of his children. The tailor would give each of the girls one hundred common pins a week and they would have to give them back at the end of the week. If she had the money, Mum used to buy toasted semechkas, sunflower seeds, a little cup for a penny. As an apprentice she didn't earn any money but had food and shelter. Back at her father's house she met Daddy. Mother could make everything from underwear to fur coats. She did alterations because making clothes didn't make any money.

We moved to Jamaica Plain because Daddy didn't want to work for Mother's family anymore. They found out about Hyde Square Tailoring where the man had died and the widow wanted to sell the business. We lived across the street on the third floor over the barbershop. There was another tenant on the second floor. We had a boarder, a Jewish man, one of lots of boarders in those years, who had a bedroom in the back. They needed the money.

Mother used to go to Mother's School with Blossom and me. It was a school to teach the immigrant women how to speak English. Teacher used to say, "Mrs. Gorfinkel will speak good English because you ask questions." She went in the daytime. We were very young. The barber who owned the building used to talk about people all the time. Apparently he owed my parents money so he cut Blossom's and my hair. We just wanted a trim and daddy wasn't satisfied with the cut so he told the barber to give us a real haircut and not listen to us. He did a bowl cut. When I saw it I wouldn't go to school. I cried for three days and I never went back to a barber in my life.

Mother was such a generous person. Daddy used to say for such a hard worker, she spent it very fast. Nothing was too good for any of us, even when we were married. She

never wanted anything for herself. Whenever we brought
her a gift, the next person who walked in the door got the
gift. She never kept anything for five minutes. She gave
me every bottle of perfume customers brought her, but I
never used it either, so it turned to alcohol in five years and
I threw it out then.

She gave all her clothes away, and even when she had
only a few things to wear, she'd give them away and buy
new ones. Mum told me more than once, "The dress that I
would like has never been made." She never found a dress
that she thought was super for her. She never made clothes
for herself although she did make a sari into a dress for you
to wear at the Ball at Brandeis. I remember it, lavender and
gold, from fabric brought by Jeannie from India for you.
I also remember that when I was fourteen and went to my
first New Year's party for boys and girls at a lovely house
in Roxbury, Mum made me a champagne velvet dress that
was gorgeous. She had only one customer, a very good
customer, that she made clothes for. But she never made
clothes for herself. She got all her pleasure from doing
things for others, especially her three children.

Celia and Evelyn with other models at a fashion show.

Part Two

Her Legacy

Miriam, 5, and Blossom, 3,
in fur coats and hats made by Celia.

Section Four

Values

I think the most important legacy our mother left us was her strong commitment to values. She believed so deeply in love and caring, in hard work and sharing, in education and giving back, that we absorbed these lessons as children. Then, when we had our own children, we passed them on without a conscious decision to do so. It was just the way it was. They say that you never know what you have taught your children until you see the way they teach theirs; now we know. We see our grandchildren following the same paths, either working in or working toward fields in which people are served by their talents and energy.

It's Black or It's White
Honesty

She looked at the hair clip in my six-year-old hand.
"Where did you get that, darling?" she asked.
I smiled at her, for I loved her and I loved the hair clip.
"In the store, " I said.

"And how did you pay for it, Love?"

"I just took it, Mamatchka."

"Well, we'll have to go back to the store and return it," she said. "It isn't right to take anything that isn't yours unless you pay for it. Then it's yours."

Sharing

My friend and I were playing dolls.

"She grabbed!" I wailed.

"Just let her have it for a little while," said my mother. "One hand washes another."

When Julie was tired of my doll she returned it and offered me one of hers to play with for a little while.

Respect for Parents

We were playing horse and rider, my middle sister and I. I was frustrated because she was older, bigger, bossy, and I always had to be the horse.

"I want to ride," I yelled.

"Children," my mother called, " your father is sleeping."

We continued playing, but the horse and rider were whispering now.

Loyalty

Daddy died at fifty-eight and my mother was still a young, vibrant woman. Men called her, brought her flowers, and asked her to go out with them. But she just continued working at her sewing machine, telling stories, singing, laughing at the thought of a "date."

"No, Babele," she chuckled. "I had a husband. I have a family. I believe in one God, one man, one family. I am happy."

Her commandments were not orders. They were given as gifts, markers to lead the way. We learned, my sisters

and I, about honesty, about respect, about loyalty, about
friendship, about sharing. She talked English with a
Russian-Yiddish accent, in the universal language of love.

My Passion

Freedom is my passion. I was raised on the concept.

"Babele," my mother used to say, "look at this beautiful
country. I don't have to be afraid of policemen. There are
no soldiers breaking down the doors. No one will hurt me
or my precious three children. I can be a Jew or not. And
you, my beautiful Babele, you can go to school and be
President of the United States."

Freedom was my mother's lover. I grew up loving
everything she did. I loved the safety we felt and the opportunity I had. I loved the freedom to be educated, even
though I was female and Jewish. In her little shtetl in
Russia, her education stopped at grade six. Then, at age
eleven, she was apprenticed to a dressmaker so she could
learn a trade and make clothes for the family she would
surely have. But here, she reminded me, I could be
anything I wanted to be.

During the McCarthy era I felt my first stirrings of fear.
I worried that my liberal attitude would cause my family
grief. I was at college and the students were marching.
Some of us were going to meetings where speakers spoke
up for socialism. The "C" word then was communism,
not cancer. I was frightened because I could relate to the
speakers who sounded so much like my father, and because I believed what they were saying. I thought it sounded fair to spread the wealth. Why should people be hungry
in a land of plenty, in beautiful America? I didn't march,
but I did listen. It was a fearful time. I was angry that our
precious freedom was at stake and that people who spoke
up were blacklisted. It was a dangerous time.

During the Bush administration I was angry again. The freedom I cherished was at risk. It was unpopular to dissent with this administration. It is considered unpatriotic to be anti-war. Was it also dangerous? As our civil rights were battered in the name of security, were we exposing our precious freedom to erosion?

Unlike what I believed as a child, I have learned that freedom is not a constant, even in our society. It must be fought for and won in every generation. We must guard the right to dissent, the right to question. Even as we hate war and its needless young deaths, we can love our country. We can be anti-war without being anti-American. We can be pro-war without being a warmonger. But we cannot be free Americans if we are not able to express our opinions without fear.

I believe that losing our freedom is the greatest danger we face. It is a greater danger than terrorism and a greater danger than a Saddam Hussein. We didn't need a Saddam to enslave us. We will do it to ourselves if we lose our passion for freedom.

Give Until It Hurts

I hated Sunday afternoons when I was a little girl growing up in Jamaica Plain, Massachusetts. There was nothing to do in the neighborhood because all the kids were with their large, happy families, or so it seemed to us. They all had dozens of cousins, grandparents, things to do at church, and places to go. And my two sisters and I had no extended family, no cousins, no grandparents, nobody out there just waiting to see us. Daddy's family had never "come over" from Russia and mother's family – her brothers and a sister – had come over, but not one member of the family talked to any other member. And her parents were dead in the old country.

So there we were, full of the good food mother always provided, but bored with each other and with ourselves. We were itching to go somewhere, anywhere but where we were. Secretly, we all hoped it would be to the Farm, but we always said anywhere would be fine. Daddy, exhausted from his week's work and aching with arthritis, was stretched out on the couch, sleeping. Mother, equally exhausted from her eighteen-hour days, was struggling to stay awake and pay attention to us. We were untouched by their weariness, not being a bit weary ourselves, and we were merciless.

"Let's DO something," we'd whine. "Let's GO somewhere."

Daddy slept on, and mother would sigh. "Oy, Mayer-ke," she'd whisper. "Wake up. The children want to take a ride."

"Later, Lichtich," he'd say to the light of his life. "Later."

We'd whine, she'd whisper, he'd stir and mumble, and finally he'd give up and put on his hat and coat, signaling to us that we were going for a ride.

In no time at all we were on our way, piled into the Pierce Arrow motorcar, heading down the Worcester Turnpike towards the Hood's Farm, an hour and a half away. Today it takes less than an hour, but then highways were rougher and cars were slower. I was convinced that daddy had to take his hat off, for if he were wearing a hat, a policeman would come along and pinch him, which was the way people described getting a ticket.

He tried to reassure me he was safe from the policemen, even with a hat, as long as he didn't speed, but I couldn't be convinced. So all the way to Hood's, I stood on the floor behind him, yanking the hat off his head, as he patiently put it back on. The miracle is that he could drive at all.

The conversation all the way to the Farm was about what we would order to eat when we got there. There were cows and other animals, a silo (whatever that was), and vast acres of farmland to be seen at Hood's, but our only interest was in the building that looked like a giant milk bottle, the wonderful place where they served warm chocolate cake and creamy ice cream.

We always ordered the same thing no matter what we said on the way, and each of us would walk away from the window with the fudge cake, vanilla ice cream, and hot gooey fudge sauce which stuck to the plate as we scooped up the cake and ice cream. On the way home we sang songs, and content with the food and the trip, we even slept.

When I think now of those Sunday rides and realize how brutally tired my parents must have been, I wish I could tell them I'm sorry. But I think that they knew how much it meant to us to do something as a family on Sunday, so they reached deep into themselves to give us that pleasure. I hope they enjoyed it, too.

Symphony Rush

TGIF was our freedom cry before it became a restaurant. At Simmons College, on the Fenway in Boston, we were close enough to Symphony Hall to catch the Friday matinee if we ran there right after our last Friday class. Students could buy rush seats for $1.00, and we were young enough to trudge the two flights of stairs up into the last rows of the balcony.

The distance from Simmons to Symphony was about a mile, so we'd be out of breath when we got there, but elated that we had made it before all the tickets were gone, with five minutes left to enjoy the view.

Ah, the view. No, I don't mean our bird's eye view of the elegantly dressed Boston matrons, hatted and gloved, demurely picking their way into the front rows of the orchestra. I don't even mean the fun of watching the latecomers pretending they were not really late by walking slowly in front of the people who grudgingly stood and allowed them to pass, rude as they were.

No, the real view was at eye level all around us, white marble statues of Greek and Roman gods and goddesses, magnificent in their size and elegance in the niches to the right and left of us. We gave the Goddesses short shrift. After all, we knew all we needed to know about what women looked like.

But the gods were another matter. Perhaps they wouldn't have been as fascinating to girls who had fathers and brothers, but I grew up in a matriarchy, and had never seen a nude male. My mother, who never liked to talk about sex, surely hadn't enlightened me.

Here they were, our companions for two hours, our unobstructed view accompanied by the glorious music of Boston Symphony, and we could stare to our heart's content. No wonder they called it "Symphony Rush"!

Our graduation was scheduled for the Simmons field hockey grounds, or at Symphony Hall if it rained. To my delight it rained, and in cap and gown I could receive my diploma under the friendly eyes of my gods, clothed only in their luminescent marble.

But, on the orchestra level, the magic was gone. As we hesitation-walked down the aisle onto the stage, I picked up my head to say Hello. There they were, but remote, small, disinterested in the graduates. They might as well have been robed in velvet. No longer muscled, nude gods, they were just marble statues. I had deserted them, and they were deserting me.

Advice

Do you think "vice" is in the word "advice" for no reason? Can you think of anything else people would rather give than receive? Even before a friend of ours begins to tell about a problem she is having, Dotty has the answer.

"I know exactly what you should do," she smiles, nodding her head wisely.

The word 'should' is a warning. It's a showstopper. It implies that Dotty knows the answer and our friend, even though she's a lovely person, doesn't have a clue. But Dotty does. Of course she does. She's been there. She knows. She has learned from her many experiences and she is more than willing to share her insights with anyone who will listen. It seems irrelevant to Dotty that someone may not want her advice when she is so willing to give it and obviously knows the answers.

Why this diatribe on advice? It stems from my earliest years of marriage, when I inherited, along with a wonderful husband and charming mother-in-law, an irascible father-in-law who downloaded free advice from a generous heart and gifted mind. What he didn't have was the radar that would have told him his advice was neither wanted nor well received by his naïve, inexperienced daughter-in-law.

He peppered his visits with "you need," "you should have," and ended with "I'll get it for you," totally unaware that I'd rather have gone with nothing than have him impose his taste and his largesse on us while we were finding our way into marriage. I didn't want to hurt his feelings so I accepted his gifts, keeping things I really didn't like, and becoming more and more resistant to his counsel.

What a lesson in giving and receiving. I'm sure I turned down some really good advice, just because I was feeling demeaned. That's when it came to me. Unsolicited advice is a putdown. The giver feels powerful and the receiver feels powerless.

My advice? Don't give it unless you're asked, and even then, be gentle, not generous.

Spirituality

She talked to God and knew where to find Him. But I don't. Where is spirituality? How do I find it? I know my body. I know its strengths and its weaknesses. I know how to nurture it and how to spoil it. I think I know it better than my doctors do, for who has the heartburn, who the labor pains, who the runny nose, who the leg cramps? Who exults after an aerobic workout in the pool? Who relishes the deep breathing during meditation?

I know my brain a bit. I know its strengths and weaknesses. I cherish its ability to cut through confusion, to absorb new knowledge, to produce divergent thoughts, to stay with a problem, poking at its insides until the juice flows free. I struggle with its inability to hold onto names or numbers, to recall times and places, to divulge data long stored in its inner recesses.

I know almost nothing about my soul. I do love its loving, its willingness to share, its concern for the weak and the frightened, its ability to forgive. I'm not satisfied with its weaknesses, its impatience, its too narrow vision, its discomfort with the unfamiliar.

And where is the spirit? Is it within the body, the brain or the soul? Or is it a separate thing, there to be served but not observed? Can I find it in dreams, in the woods, on a hillside, down at the lake? If I block out the world, quiet the brain, slow down the body, soothe the soul, will the spirit present itself to me? And if I then hold it in my hands and look into its face, will I know its name?

If spirituality is the love, the concern, the tenderness

that rises in me, then I am spiritual. If it is the tingling appreciation of the beauty in the world, then I am spiritual. If it is the sense of kinship I feel with people, then I am spiritual. If it is my connection to my mother and her connection to God, then I am spiritual. And if it is none of these, then I am still searching.

Reverence

Every Rosh Hashanah and Yom Kippur since I can remember, I have sat in temple and read the prayer book for the High Holy Days in Hebrew and in English. "On the First Day of the Year it is written and on the Day of Atonement it is sealed, who shall live, who shall die, who by stoning, who by . . . but penitence, prayer, and charity shall avert the severe decree."

I have been through stages in my religious life, just as I have been in my social, economic, intellectual, personal, political, public and private lives, and as I write this I recall a few. As a child I read the Book and believed it because my mother did. I tried to be penitent, prayerful, and charitable. I think, too, there was an element of superstition in it for me. Perhaps if I am really good I will ward off the evil eye that's watching us. I'll be so good that no one, not even the Almighty, will get me.

Then I recall the college years when we played bridge for hours in the dark, smoke-filled lounge next door to the boiler, stopping only long enough between rubbers to ask questions.

"Is there a God?"

"Why do Catholics believe . . .?"

"Why do Jews believe . . .?"

"Why do Protestants believe?"

If the questions got serious enough, we'd stop the game, drink coffee, smoke cigarettes, and seriously explore the meaning of life, never caring about answers, just relishing the discussions.

Then I married and had children. The birth of a child, a marvelous small being in the image of its father and mother. Here was surely an answer to the Big Question. Somebody, something, some Being had to be responsible for this miracle. Was this child in the heavenly ledger as well? Was his/her name written, then sealed? What did he or she know of penitence, prayer, and charity? Or did that only apply to people old enough to read, to pray, to understand? As I grew older, raised children, lost parents, lost intimate friends, changed lifestyles, I continued to go to temple on those High Holy Days, continued to read, to question, to wonder.

It had never been hard for me to be charitable, since it was a value instilled by my mother in particular and my culture in general. I had never had difficulty with penitence if that meant being sorry for being bad. If I hurt someone, or if I inadvertently or even willfully made someone else very unhappy, I always felt sorry for that. I tried not to repeat that fault. But prayer? Only in temple, and then with halfhearted attention, for the meaning of the words was more interesting to me than the act of prayer. To Whom was I praying? But the words haunted me. "On the first day of the year it is written . . ." How I have wondered about those words when I have seen good, kind, charitable, even prayerful people die too young, become too ill, or become inconsolably bitter because of life's blows.

The urge to be fatalistic is strong. Perhaps, I thought, nothing really makes a difference. It is written and that's all there is to it. And now today I sit in the doctor's office waiting to hear if a lesion in my eye has changed since he looked at it last. We hear the diagnosis. It's fine. I take my husband's arm as we walk back to the car, filled with relief and gratitude, remembering the sadness in a man's face as he came out of the office. Who shall live and who shall die?

"I'm going home and give to charity," I say. I wonder if I'll pray.

Patience

It's been a lifelong struggle, this business of learning patience. Even as I watched my mother sitting at her sewing machine, endlessly pushing fabric through the needle, always smiling as she worked, even with that example, I was impatient.

I could never wait for my birthday or for the fresh rolls my mother brought from the bakery. I couldn't wait for the fun, the food, the companionship. I was always anticipating, rarely appreciating the moment because my sights were always on the future. When would the next good time come?

And the day, as all days do, would come. The party would be fun, but the day would end and tears would wash over my face because it was over. Now I'd have to be patient and wait for the next happy time. The rolls would come. We'd cover them with cream cheese, wash them down with cold milk, and then they would be gone.

I'd sit on the fence at camp, waiting for my mother to arrive on Visiting Day. I could barely sit still as car after car drove up, always someone else's parents. My patience stretched to its limits, there she would be, smiling at me, gathering me into her full bosoms, and telling me how much she loved me. All would be well and Visiting Day would be over, and then I'd be back to waiting again, this time for the daycamp to end and she would come to pick me up.

But the wedding day, scheduled right after college

Ceil picked him and I kept him.

graduation, would that day really come? I knew it would and the day would end. What would happen to the world, I wondered, when that day would come and go? Would the world still be there, with us in it, married? And assuming it all happened, still a world, still us in it, what would we then talk to each other about, forever?

Of course it came, the world moved on, and we are still talking. But now I find that there is often no need to talk. We understand each other without words. I am no longer impatient for time to pass. I relish the moments, watching our middle-aged children grow older, our grandchildren growing up, us growing old together. We savor the years, the months, the days, the moments. I have all the patience in the world.

"What a difference a day makes," my mother used to say.

Pride Goeth before a Fall

"Buena Park, CA" said the return address.

"My publisher!" I yelled. "She sent me the cover of the book."

My husband, as excited as I, opened it up and there it was, *Teen Moms: the Pain and the Promise* in handsome colors, black, yellow, red, white and pink. PAIN shivered in red, the PROMISE was calm in quiet yellow. The rose at the bottom left opened its petals in glowing pink, and the EVELYN LERMAN in white, leaped up from the bottom right side of the cover. I choked with the thrill of seeing my own book cover come to life. No book yet, but what a gorgeous start. Talk about promise!

In his usual efficient manner, Allie took the cover from me and headed right to the framer so he could hang it on the wall.

Then, almost as an afterthought, he said, "I noticed your right front tire is going flat, so we'll take it to the tire place this afternoon."

The mechanic jacked up the car on the apron of the shop and disappeared into the garage to repair the tire. It was a drizzly, dreary day in Sarasota and the garage had no waiting room or ladies' room, so I began walking around on the tarmac to make time pass. Lost in the joy of my book cover, I tripped on the jack handle, flew over it and onto the macadam, chin first, elbows second, and knees last. Blood spurted from all areas, especially the mouth. My lower teeth had bitten through my upper lip.

Twelve stitches later, abrasions dressed, legs bandaged, and filled with aspirin and TLC, I opened my eyes.

Allie looked down at me, that worried expression I know so well. "What were you thinking about, Ev?" he asked.

"My book cover," I whispered. I tried to grin but the swelling and the stitches got in the way.

"My book cover," I sighed.

The Recurring Dream

People call me obsessive because I rarely leave my work undone. Whether it's a lesson plan or a shopping list, I always try to finish it before I go to bed. What they don't know about me is that not only do I have the strong work ethic instilled by my mother, I also have a fear. I know that if I don't do what I think needs doing, I'll have the Recurring Dream.

I'm running through the school corridors looking for
the room I'm supposed to be in. I'm late and I'm lost. It's
there in the corner, the room with all the windows. Re-
lieved, I look in, but the room is filled with people who do
not belong in my class. Of course, it's the room just be-
neath this one on the second floor. I head for the stairs, the
book bag getting heavier as I run. But the stairs don't lead
directly to the second floor. They take me to the bridge,
which connects with the next building.

If I had a schedule and a map of the building, I'd be
fine. So I look for the sign that says "Office." The Office is
as elusive as the classroom and I spend precious minutes
prowling the corridors. The bag gets heavier. My legs get
tired. It gets later and later. I scrape my knee against the
brick interior wall as I squeeze past groups of students who
know where they are going.

Now I run. I'm hot and thirsty, hungry and tired. I'm
late. My dry mouth wakes me. As I gulp water, I put the
dream away for another night.

Every Ring Is a Year

The wooden slab sat heavily on the brass stand, throwing its full weight on it, two inches thick from the side,
three feet across the top. Lacquered and glazed, it glowed,
smooth to the touch on the surface, rough-barked on
the outside.

"Every ring's a year," the old farmer told me when I
stopped to watch him cookie cutting the huge tree trunk
with his chain saw. "Yep, this here tree's been in the family
over 200 years. Would've been here longer hadn't been
struck by lightning. Take a slab home with you. Keep
you humble seeing how much longer a tree can live
than people."

I smile, more a chuckle than a smile. He was the

Mainer I'd come to expect when I got off the highways into the country roads in central Maine. "You know the history of this tree?" I asked.

"Sure do. My old man grew up on this farm. His father before him, and his old man before him. Tree was planted when my great-great grandfather had his first-born. Wanted to do something for the boy. Let the child have something to grow up to. Wasn't long before the oak outgrew the kid in height and in width. Stood 100 feet tall when it got struck. Lucky it fell to the North. If it fell the other way would've crushed the house, the barn, and all of us in it." He shrugged, put the saw down carefully, respectfully, and patted the tree trunk. "Don't 'magine we have much to say about it. Act of the Lohhd. Been my time to go, he'd have heaved it the other way. Didn't. So I guess I've got a few more years to put in on this earth. Here. Take a slab. Remind you of who guides us."

I offered to pay him, but he shrugged me off. "Don't need no pay. Just take it home and put it somewhere you'll remember the way it looked before I cut it up."

He hauled the slice of oak to my wagon, grunting under the weight of it as he slid it into the wayback.

"Thanks very much!" I called out as I drove off. The chain saw was back at work, the farmer watching its teeth cut into the next slice.

I found the old brass stand in my attic, encouraged my husband to shellac the top of the slab, and we put the oak coffee table on our screened porch. Smooth on the surface, rough on the edges, over 200 years old. Anytime I get too full of myself, I start counting the rings. Keeps me humble.

Sexy Grandma

"You can tell my grandma anything," said Lori. "She even brought me a condom holder from the Netherlands

when I was only thirteen!"

I stood in the store, admiring the display of sex equipment. Only in the Netherlands would an older-than-middle aged woman find such an array, and only in the Netherlands would she feel comfortable buying any of it. It wasn't arranged to titillate or to elicit the WOW! factor. It was there to educate and inspire safe sex habits. That's what I was there for, in preparation for writing a book about teenage mothers, and what we in the United States had to do about it.

As I looked over the materials I thought about my grandchildren, aged 7, 14, 16, and 23.

"Whoa," I thought. Except for Becca and Jerry, they are the age of the teen mothers I've been interviewing; they are at risk and may not even know it. Our sex education in the States is so restrictive. I knew I didn't have to worry about the 23-year old. She was way ahead of me in everything. The seven-year-old was still young. But I was sure it was time for my son and daughter-in-law to talk seriously with their teenagers about sex and unsafe sex. Perhaps they had, but perhaps they hadn't. In any case, my gifts would surely stimulate some kind of discussion.

So I bought three tube-shaped condom holders in the Dutch reproductive health clinic and spent many hours on the plane trip home figuring out how to give them to the younger grandchildren. As is usual for me, when I worry a lot about something, no ideas come. But when I lay back, ideas fall into my lap. Sure enough, when I got back to camp, I took Lori out for our annual night of stargazing while lying on a blanket in the soccer field.

She had just returned from her girls' camp and it was Father/Son weekend at Caribou. Two women in a boys' camp filled with campers and their fathers had to find their own amusement, so we had a perfect night for our outing.

"It's hard being a girl in a boys' camp, Grandma," she said.

There it was. We talked about being girls, but I didn't touch the idea of safer sex or any kind of sex, figuring it wasn't mine to do. But I had the opener for my discussion with her mom. The next day Martha told me she and Lori had a wonderful discussion about girls and sex, about waiting until you are ready, about safety and health. Lori assured her mother that she's not ready. Even though there are kids in high school having sex, her crowd doesn't think it's a good idea.

Years later I asked Lori what she thought about the condom holder that her mom gave her as a gift from Grandma. She laughed. She had no idea what it was because it was a tube, and wasn't shaped like any condom she had ever seen.

A Piece of Music

If I were a piece of music, I'd be the "1812 Overture." I'd have to be Russian because I was raised by a strong Russian woman. She was larger than life, and she offered me the same opportunity.

I'd have to be melodious, but I'd have to be strident, too. I'd have all the rhythm and harmony of the orchestra at its warmest, and all the clanging and banging of the orchestra at its most dramatic.

No quiet, four-piece chamber music for me, so constrained, so delicate, so polite and reverent. No, I'd need to be a piece of music that bent and soared, uncowed and triumphant, that cooperated and competed, polite and passionate.

I'd need a lovely start and an "in your face" ending.

I'm here, I'm loving, I'm soft, I'm loud, says the Overture, and that's only the beginning.

The Senses

My mother was all about mind and body. Education came first, but right after that came good, plentiful, tasty food. Once those needs were satisfied, she devoted her spirit to the sun, the feel of fabric in her hands, the wonderful smell of freshly baked raised dough, the sights of beautiful people and things and the wondrous sounds of nature. She was aware of her senses all the time, even as she worked. We grew up smothered by her love and her awareness, and I see her again in our grandchildren in their appreciation of life's best moments.

It's a Wonderful World

As I grow older with my enthusiasm for life and my optimistic ability to solve problems undiminished, I thank my earth mother who raised me to believe that it's a wonderful world. Her eyes were always on the sky, looking beyond the fire escape outside the dining room window to the patch of blue sky it framed.

When I questioned her about that, she'd answer, "I talk to God."

Somehow I think her discussions with God were wrapped up in her appreciation for the five senses, though we knew she had a sixth sense as well. That intuitive sense may have been her ability to throw the other senses together, or her appreciation for everything that went on around her.

We were raised to listen to the smell of the pines as we drove through New Hampshire heading for summer camp.

"Hehr vee ess schmecht. Hear how it smells," Mother would say.

We never questioned whether you could listen to a smell, but would breathe deeply, listen attentively, and as we heard the wind rustle through the trees, we'd smell the pines along with her.

In her sewing room filled with the racks of clothing she was fixing for her customers, she'd say, "See how the garments feel. All the different fabrics."

And I'd run my hands over the velvets and cottons and silks and I'd say, "I see."

When we'd smell the fresh challah at the table, and we'd cut the honeydew melon into quarters for the four of us, she'd hand each of us the braided bread and say, "Break off a piece."

No knife, just pull off a piece any size you like, and as the piece of the braid filled your hands, you'd smell the bread with your fingers and hear it crunch with your eyes.

She knew all, heard all, saw all, She used her six senses all the time, and she used them for our benefit. If we were sad, she knew it; if we were happy, she rejoiced. No matter how little money we had or how difficult the times were, she was in our midst filled with the wonder and beauty of the world, giving us hugs and a groaning table of good food along with hot baths and warm clothing. She withheld nothing, giving us all the love, all the food, and all the time she had to share.

When she died she left each of us a sewing machine, a few hundred dollars, and the ability to enjoy life, even in its smallest moments.

Plain Vanilla

Ice cream is my favorite food, even plain vanilla. It's my first ice cream memory, and it may have triggered my lifetime longing for ice cream. Just so you know, I'd rather have a mocha ice cream soda than breakfast. I'd rather have a hot fudge sundae than lunch. And I'd rather have a towering soft serve, black and white cone than supper. I don't, but I'd rather.

Back to vanilla, when it all started. I was probably four years old, sitting in a hospital bed, trying to swallow, but only succeeding in crying. Even that hurt because the tonsillectomy was so recent. A starched, white-hatted nurse, carrying a tray on which sat a cylindrical box, the kind ice cream stores used to put a pint of scooped ice cream into, interrupted my misery. She smiled as she handed me the box with a spoon.

I was confused because whatever was in the box seemed like it was too much for one person. "All for me?" I asked her.

"All for you," she smiled, tying a towel around my neck and bringing the tray table closer to me.

I opened the box to find a tightly packed, smooth topped, pint of vanilla ice cream.

"Guaranteed to soothe the pain," she said.

I began dipping. It was smooth, cold, rich, sweet, and all mine. By the time I finished it, and finish it I did, my throat was frozen, desensitized, and pain free.

I was hooked.

Taste

The writing assignment in my class was "Taste." I didn't head for the spice cabinet. I didn't even treat myself to a guilt-free spree, eating the assignment, per order of the teacher. All I had to do was remember every ice cream parlor of my youth, because my taste for cold ice cream and hot fudge remains as sharp and demanding as ever. I love it, I want it, I even crave it. I can still have the ice cream, but not the fudge sauce. Yes, I can go to Delites and have phony ice cream and ersatz hot fudge, thus eliminating the cholesterol, but it's not the same.

So let me share my ice cream parlors with you, from fair to fabulous.

On the corner of our block stood St. Clair's, a gathering place for ladies having lunch and an occasional spot for the younger crowd. We couldn't afford the whole meal, but we could indulge in a hot fudge sundae now and then. It must have been just OK, because I can't really describe it, except to say that the dish was glass and tulip-shaped. The sundae I don't remember.

Then there was Friendly's. The ice cream was creamy when it wasn't icy, and the fudge was a pudding-like consistency, which dribbled around the ice cream. But the sauce got cold too fast and the ice cream melted too fast, so only the first few bites made it.

Priscilla Alden was a few blocks away, but worth the walk. Not for the ice cream, which was good but not exceptional, but for the hot fudge which was special. It was dark and thick and sticky with an aftertaste as good as the taste. So good, in fact, that one night when our group descended there en masse, I ordered just plain hot fudge, no ice cream. It was a teenage boast. I can eat a whole sundae dish of straight hot fudge, I told them, and they took me up on it. They watched me gag through the whole orgy. No doubt this was the beginning of my intolerance for rich food.

Brigham's was still further away, a good mile down Beacon Street, but we were happy to make the trip. The ice cream was marvelous, especially the mocha almond. The fudge sauce was thick, rich, hot, sticky, and lasted throughout the sundae. And the sundaes were huge because our friend Ellie worked there and piled our plates high. We judged our Brigham's the best in Brookline.

But – if you were willing to take the streetcar to town and get off at the Park Street stop, there was Bailey's. We had the sundae instead of lunch so we wouldn't feel guilty about eating it. By that time Ellie and I were into size 16s, possibly 18s, and beginning to think we might be getting fat. So the sundae substituted for lunch. The ice cream? A perfect vanilla, smooth, creamy. The fudge? Black, rich, dense, dripping down the ice cream very slowly. It dripped onto the tin plate, which held the tin sundae dish. You started at the plate, scraping your way up to the bowl, and then finally digging into the mountain of ice cream covered with fudge sundae. It was delicious. It was hot and cold, sweet and creamy, gorgeous and elegant. We loved the sundae, each other and life. We were at the apex of self-indulgence. As we licked our spoons we decided it was time to consider a serious diet. Next time, we agreed, we would forego both breakfast and lunch before having our Bailey's sundae.

A Taste, a Memory

A mocha frappe transports me. I'm eleven years old, at 1862 Beacon Street, in a second floor walkup apartment, where I grew to twenty-one. We had moved from Jamaica Plain, an Irish Catholic neighborhood, to Brookline, a middle- to upper-middle class neighborhood where, my mother assured me, I would meet a nice Jewish boy. Like so many of her predictions, she got that right, too.

So here we were, with me going to a new school, where I was no longer the only Jew among Irish Catholics; I was the only poor Jew among what was then called "comfortable" Jews and Gentiles.

I made my way to the new school, across the streetcar tracks from our neighborhood, and there I felt as isolated as I had felt in my old school, down the street from St. Mary's Church. Everyone else was dressed in pleated skirts with long, matching cashmere sweaters, bobby sox and saddle shoes. And then I saw her, Ellie, a tall, blonde girl, smiling at me. She looked more like me than anyone else did, and she was friendly.

So, where's the frappe? At Ellie's house, the place we went to every day after school. There was Ellie's stay-at-home mom, in the kitchen. And there was the magical eggbeater, which sat in a Mason jar with a top. Into that quart jar Mae put milk, chocolate syrup and coffee ice cream she bought at Morgan's Creamery. Mae whirled the beater energetically, frothing up this delicious concoction, and Ellie and I drained the jug every afternoon.

The cold, the chocolate, the coffee, the creamy texture on the tongue, nothing beats a mocha frappe, even today. Although I rarely give myself the opportunity because the calorie count is obscene, the memory lingers: it was friendship; it was comfort; it was acceptance; it was love.

Always Cinnamon

Always cinnamon. It's not important what's cooking or baking. As long as it's cinnamon I want to eat it. My first

memories go back to childhood when my mother's friend
Lizzie brought her homemade cinnamon rolls to the weekly poker game. The smell was overwhelming because she
brought them hot, and I could taste the smell even before
I ate it. I was ravenous as always, never full, and always
ready for more, especially those huge raised dough
cinnamon rolls that tore apart when you ate them.

A more recent memory? The real estate agent told me,
when we were selling our home before moving to Florida,
"When you show the house, be sure to have an apple pie
baking in the oven. Lots of cinnamon."

I didn't have the time or the inclination or even the
talent to make a pie, so I cut up apples, drowned them in
cinnamon and sugar, and put them into the oven to bake.
Whether it was location, or the market, or the cinnamon,
twelve days of baked apples later, we sold the house.

Cinnamon, I love you still.

Peanut Butter and Tears

"June Brown. 1925 to 2004. Beloved Mother, Wife,
Grandmother." I stopped at the headstone, a sharp intake
of breath surprising me as I read. June Brown, dead.
Seventy years earlier we had lived in the same cabin in
a girls' camp.

I had pretended I was asleep when I heard them getting
out of bed. Whatever they were up to was wrong, I knew.
There would be trouble, and the only thing worse than not
being part of the group was being part of the group when
they were in trouble. Fat was one thing; disobedient was
another. But I also knew that not being part of the group
would make me even more of an outsider than I already
was. I knew they were whispering about me, knowing I
was awake and hadn't joined them.

"Scaredy cat. Teacher's pet." They had other names for

me and those were the kindest.

I shrank my body together, scrunched my chubby legs into my protruding stomach, hiding myself under the covers. The other eight-year-olds in the bunk were huddled together on the wooden floor, whispering, muffling their giggles so the counselor on duty wouldn't hear them. They were breaking the rules, they knew, and it would be hard to explain to the O.D. what they were doing, eating peanut butter and saltines at midnight, hours after they were supposed to be asleep.

The smell of peanut butter overcame my fear. Maybe I'd get up after all and slip into the group to get my share. I forced myself to push the heavy woolen blankets down, pulled my flannel pajamas over my arms and legs and tip-toed onto the wooden floor, bare feet shrinking from the cold.

"Hi," I whispered, bending over an empty space in the circle. "Can I have some?"

"No way," scowled June, the leader of the group. "You're too fat already."

Hot tears rolled from my eyes into my mouth. My legs crumpled, pitching me onto the floor. I lay there, helpless, sobbing.

"God," said June, "now you've spoiled the party. The counselor is sure to hear us. Come on, girls, let's go back to bed."

June threw the peanut butter jar, the crackers, and the smeared knives into a paper bag as my bunkmates dashed to their beds. I licked my fingers to pick up the few crumbs on the floor, the salty taste mingling with my tears, and crawled back to bed. Under the covers I stifled my sobs, hoping that sleep would end my misery.

Now June was asleep forever. I was sorry we had never eaten peanut butter crackers together.

I Hear Her

When I hear the crack of an egg into a bowl, there she is, my mother-in-law, apron tucked neatly around her, baking a cake.

"Please, Jeannie," I say, "stop working and talk to me. We came to visit you in Florida, and here you are in the kitchen, working."

"So talk to me. I can work and you can talk." She cracks the egg against the side of the bowl.

"But I miss you. I want to hear how you are doing. How do you feel? How are things going with Dad?"

"How can I feel? I feel like I always feel. I'm old now. And Dad? He's the same. He pouts. He gets over it." CRACK!

She was making her eight-egg angel cake, so we had six cracks to go. Maybe then she'd stop working and talk to me. But the cake leads to the salad, the salad to the dressing, the dressing to the green beans, the vegetable to the potato. Her preparations continue.

Finally it comes to me. Nana Jeanne spoke with her eggs. Nana Ceil spoke with her needle. Together they taught me the language of life.

Touch

Elizabeth, the dressmaker's dummy, stood watch as I ran my fingers down the row of finished garments. Customers would come soon to pick them up and they would be gone – my slippery silks and smooth cottons, my deep velvets and ribbed corduroys, my sleek nylons and elusive rayons.

Two long steel racks stood side by side, one for finished clothes, the other for garments pinned by my mother, ready for her expert hands and her Singer. I avoided the pinned rack because a hidden pin could prick a finger and the blood on the garments was more lasting than the pain of the finger.

But the finished rack was mine. I touched the clothes before I left for school and ran my hands over them when I returned home. Some of my favorites would be gone, but some new ones, even some warm from the iron, would be on the rack. Thus I kept track of my Mother's busy hours, the thousands of stitches she produced during her sixteen-hour days.

Racks of clothing still beckon me. A Saks rack calls to me. I trail my fingers slowly by, stopping when something feels just right. I check the size. If it's mine, I know it without trying it on. I buy with my fingers, and with my memories.

Blossie's Noodle Pudding

My sister Blossom was a foodie, long before we knew the word, and long before chefs cooked on television. In fact, she was a foodie before we had television. She was a wonderful cook, baker, party giver and hostess.

When my two sisters and I were married and had children we determined that we would celebrate every holiday, both secular and religious, with a get-together dinner. We were adamant because we hadn't had extended family as children and we had really missed grandparents, aunts, uncles and cousins. My working mother and my sick father did everything they could to make our Sundays and holidays special, but we were lonesome. So we agreed that the holidays for our children would be filled with food and family.

We'd meet some weeks before the event to agree on the menu and to parcel out the work. No matter the main course, we always had Blossie's noodle pudding. Now that could have been the end of that discussion except for the fact that my oldest sister Miriam was a dietitian and a health foodie. She was slim and trim and Blossom was a bit hefty, as one might expect from their food preferences. Mimi would say, "Blossie, you make your noodle pudding and I'll make mine."

So they each brought theirs, Blossom's tall and round in a 10-inch spring form and Mimi's long and thin in an 8 x 12-inch baking dish. Blossie's pudding was filled with the ingredients you'll see in the recipe below, and Mimi's was the low fat, low sugar version. You can guess which pudding disappeared.

An interesting coda to this story is that Blossom's son Robert became a chef and perfected her noodle pudding. He still makes it to this day.

Blossie's Noodle Pudding Recipe

Use 9" spring form, greased
Preheat oven to 350 degrees
Bake for 11/2 to 2 hours
Cook package of 10 oz. wide egg noodles, drain.
Mix in mixer:
1 lb. cottage cheese
1/2 lb. farmer's cheese
1/4 lb. cream cheese
1 cup milk
1 cup sour cream
6 eggs
1/2 cup sugar
4 Tbs. melted butter
1/2 tsp. vanilla
Fold mixture and noodles together.
Pour into pan.
Top with 2 Tbs. brown sugar, 2 Tbs. butter, 1/4 cup broken walnuts, mixed together.

Refrigerate several hours before baking – if you have the time!

Bake. Let stand before cutting into twelve wedges.

Blossie's Brisket

It was rare to see my mother cooking in the kitchen. We'd marvel that she left her sewing machine and was actually making something in a big pot. It was her signature dish and it was awful. She called it "floomen mit kartofle," and we shuddered every time she made it. But she was so proud of it that we all pretended it was good.

If we didn't actually see her in the kitchen we knew she was there by the smell. It was the dense smell of brisket combined with the cloying sweetness of the prunes. I don't think the potatoes smelled at all, but I'd know what was cooking and I wondered whether this time I could fish out the meat and ignore the prunes and potatoes. The brisket would be soft, tasty and chewy at the same time, but the prunes would be a black mush and the potatoes would be a brown mush. I decided I had to learn to make brisket without the accompaniments.

When I began cooking in my own home I discovered that my sister Blossom's brisket, like all of her cooking, was wonderful. Everything she touched, from her rich chicken soup to her brisket, to her cheesecake – all of it was delicious. She had no thought of salt or fat or richness or calories. She just thought of wonderful taste, texture, and above all, smell. If the smell was just right, so was the brisket. So I learned how to make Blossie's brisket and it has become my signature dish.

Blossie's Brisket Recipe

One whole fresh brisket (6 to 8 pounds)
6 large yellow onions, sliced

2 cups Heinz ketchup

1 cup Reunite red wine

Lawry salt

Brown brisket on both sides in hot, large heavy aluminum covered pot.

Lay onions under brisket, reserving enough to cover the top.

Cover pan, turn down low, cook until onions begin to wilt.

Season brisket very lightly with Lawry salt.

Add ketchup and wine (stirred) to cover brisket with thick layer. (Should be the consistency of very heavy cream; if more is needed use 2:1 ratio.)

Cover; simmer 3 to 4 hours until fork pierces brisket easily.

Chill brisket in casserole container, covered tightly, overnight.

Chill gravy (with onions) in tall covered pitcher, overnight.

Next day remove fat from brisket, slice and layer overlapping slices in casserole.

Remove all fat from gravy (should be thick, yellow layer), and cover brisket with gravy and onions.

Cover tightly with Saran wrap and freeze.

When ready to serve, defrost overnight in refrigerator. Heat, covered, in 350-degree oven for about an hour or in microwave for about 30 minutes.

Dear Blossom:

Thank you, dear middle sister, not only for your great recipes, but also for toughening me up. Although I was young and naïve, I knew you were right. I wanted to be tough like you; it just wasn't in me. If a boy was nasty to me, I told you and you beat him up for me. But you didn't let me off the hook.

"Don't be a mugwump," you yelled at me. "Stand up for yourself. Speak up. Be strong."

You shamed and harassed me mercilessly, but wiser and stronger now, I thank you, even though it's too late for you to hear me.

Love,
Evelyn

To Love and To Cherish

In the 1940's young people married young, many just out of high school. Those who went on to college frequently didn't finish because they got married. It was wartime, and the lucky boys who came home married their childhood sweethearts and had children. The women, though equipped with college degrees, never thought about careers; their calling was to be wife and mother. Most of those marriages lasted, since divorce had a shameful ring to it, and even bad marriages muddled through. Good marriages were frequent, however, and I was one of the lucky ones.

The Year of Discovery

"Wear this all the time," my mother said, as she fastened a large round 'James Michael Curley for Mayor' button onto my jacket. "It will protect you."

I didn't understand what she meant exactly, but I trusted her and wore it. It surely made life easier. "Dirty Jew" and

"Christ killer" faded from the mouths of the boys, and the girls invited me to play in their games at recess. Whoever James Michael Curley was, he took care of me.

My mother smiled at me. "You'll never find a nice Jewish boy to marry if we stay here. We have to move to Brookline."

The next thing I knew we were packing. I was ten, finishing the fifth grade at the Mary E. Curley elementary school in Jamaica Plain, Massachusetts, the only Jew among my twenty-four classmates. I'd been raised to get along.

We left our double-decker on South Huntington Avenue, across the streetcar tracks from the New England Home for Little Wanderers and we moved into a railroad apartment on Strathmore Road in Brookline. No tracks in sight, but a long narrow apartment from which you could hear the commuter cars on the tracks beyond the bridge. This was the bridge we walked under, through a tunnel, and then up the stairs to Dean Road where the big, beautiful, brick homes were. Down Dean Road and around the corner we found the John D. Runkle School, a K-8 Brookline school, a world away from Mary E. Curley.

I had a hint when mother removed the Curley button. "You won't need this here," she said. "You'll find lots of Jews. And the Goyim are different. You'll be safe here."

In the sixth grade, eleven years old, I discovered what it felt like to be physically safe. No taunts, no teasing, no name-calling. But I learned there was a different kind of bias here. In JP I was a Jew among Catholics; in Brookline I was a poor Jew among rich Jews and rich Gentiles.

I didn't look right. I didn't sound right. I didn't dress right. I hadn't found my real home after all. And then, in English class, I found my soul mate, Ellie. High Episcopal, a poor relation of the famous State House architect,

Charles Bullfinch, Ellie was a WASP through and through.
She was tall and blonde and gorgeous, a bit awkward and
overweight like me, and she wore the wrong clothes and
she was lonely, too.

We laughed together over her white bread sandwiches
with the crusts cut off. We laughed over my cissel bread
sandwiches with thick cream cheese. She introduced me
to lobster and I fed her hot pastrami on rye. We thrived
on Glenn Miller, hot fudge sundaes from Brigham's, and
Maybelline mascara and eyelash curlers from the Five and
Ten. We played and studied and laughed together. And we
grew up with the discovery that soul mates don't have to
share religion or ethnicity. They only have to share love.

Birthday Engagement

My nineteenth birthday/engagement party is the kind of
memory every woman should have. Mother had invited Allie and his parents to a birthday dinner for me. I was nineteen and Allie was just back from Europe after VE day, on
his way to the West Coast from where he would be shipped
to Japan. So it was an emotional time, full of excitement
and anxiety.

I can't recall the menu or the table setting, but I know it
was Coolidge Corner's best takeout and Sears Roebuck's
best china. The room was rectangular, with a side door that
led to the hall, a double door that led to mother's sewing
room, and a small door that opened to the kitchen. The
light came from an overhead globe, so all the glamour attached to that evening came from what happened, not from
the ambiance. A large, oblong dining room table filled
the room.

The first course was a huge piece of honeydew melon,
perfectly ripe and juicy, hand picked by my mother whose
educated thumb for fruit never failed. She couldn't cook

and she didn't, but she bought the biggest and the best of everything available as she walked through Coolidge Corner. She knew everyone and everyone knew her, and when the merchants saw her coming, they couldn't have been happier. Ceil bought only the best, never asked for prices, and always had a smile and a story. Because she introduced Peek a Cheek (Pick a Chick) to take-out, they had two perfectly roasted chickens ready for her whenever she came by. For this event they probably roasted her a large turkey. If we were five people, she had a twelve-pounder so "there should always be as much left as was eaten."

I got up to take the melon plates to the kitchen and returned to find a small package, wrapped in tissue, on my dinner plate. I swallowed the lump that lodged in my throat, breathed slowly and deeply to ease the tightness in my chest, and unwrapped a diamond ring. That kind of excitement comes to you only a few times in a lifetime: when you unwrap a diamond engagement ring, when the nurse puts your newborn into your arms, when the Rabbi says, "I now pronounce you man and wife," or when the whole family is gathered around the table, children and grandchildren, for a Jewish holiday and you light the candles and sing the b'rachah together.

The rest of the meal is a blur, except for the ending. In my nineteen-year-old innocence I asked, "When are we going to get married?"

Al's father answered, "What's the matter? Have you got hot pants?"

Twenty-One

The days were too crowded, even though they were dragging. I was hot. I was cold. I was hungry. I had no appetite. The school year was ending. Graduation was coming. My job was too demanding, but I needed the money.

My working mother was too busy to get me ready for the wedding. I was too busy to get myself ready. I had to take exams, work, try on clothes, select the menu, send the invitations, return the phone calls, keep my cool and get enough sleep. I was stressed beyond my ability to cope. Something had to give.

Put off the wedding? Out of the question. We'd been engaged for two years and the waiting seemed endless. Not take exams? Also out of the question. After four years of college and with graduation approaching, I just had to finish. Only the job was expendable. I had to quit, and without the customary two-weeks' notice, even though I knew it wasn't the professional thing to do. In this case, however, my personal need to survive trumped my knowledge that the man I worked for would be very angry.

I saw Mr. B. after work in his office that Monday and explained my dilemma. I had planned to work through the second week in June, figuring with graduation the first week and the wedding the third week, I could make it through the second week at the travel agency. But now, in the third week of May, I knew I couldn't keep up the pace. I'd finish this week, I told him, and thanked him for the opportunity he'd given me to work there.

His thin lips got thinner. His narrow black eyes became slits. His breathing came faster. He cleared his throat. "PICK UP YOUR CHECK ON THE WAY OUT TODAY," he said. "This is very unprofessional with no notice. Your problems are yours, not mine." He pushed his chair back and left the room.

Tears stung my eyes as I put my things together and said goodbye to my office friends. He wasn't around when I left. Oh, well, I consoled myself. It had to be done. It's over.

But it wasn't over. When I called Simmons College a

few months later, looking for a job reference, the secretary came back to the phone with a tight voice. "Evelyn, I
checked your file and I don't think you want this reference.
Mr. B. said you were irresponsible, self-centered, unprofessional, and immature." I thanked her and agreed I didn't
want the reference.

A married woman now, I decided I'd have to live without a reference. After all, I was twenty-one, a grownup. I
could do it.

The Ring of Truth: A Fish Story

I really wanted him to wear a wedding ring. He really
didn't want to. He was a free spirit, a freshly discharged
veteran back from the real war, WWII, the big one. Re-
cruited into the Army at eighteen, sent overseas to the
European theater, twice wounded in battle, he was now
home and tougher than nails. When he was refused a beer
at the ballgame because he didn't look old enough, he
reached over the counter, grabbed the man's collar, and
shouted into his face.

"I was old enough to fight for you, you son-of-a-bitch.
I'm old enough for a beer."

Was I strong enough for this man? I loved him, I knew.
I wanted to be his wife, but would I be able to stand up to
him when he strongly believed that he was right? What if I
thought he was wrong? I hadn't been in the Army. I hadn't
fought in the trenches. I hadn't been wounded. I didn't
have his testosterone.

We talked some more about the ring.

"I'd like us both to wear one, Allie," I said. "It feels
right to me. I want people to know we're married and we
belong to each other."

He laughed. "O.K.," he said. "I'll make you a deal. You
learn how to make my mother's gefilte fish, and I'll wear

a ring."

"Gefilte fish!" I cried out, thinking how little I knew about it. But what I did know, I didn't like. You had to chop fish in a wooden bowl with a metal chopper. You had to cook fish heads. You had to spend hours with it.

I told him all that and finished with, ". . . and then it may be terrible, not nearly as good as your mother's."

"That's O.K.," he answered. "Just so you try."

I think he thought I'd be afraid, not take the dare, and he'd be ring-free. But he hadn't counted on my upbringing, my strong mother.

"You'll never know unless you ask," she told me. "You'll never succeed if you don't try. Never be afraid."

So I took a lesson with my mother-in-law-to-be. She wasn't the least bit concerned about my taking over because she expected to be making gefilte fish for all of us for years to come. Then I bought the fish. I chopped the onions. I peeled the carrots. I cooked the heads. I rolled the balls. I seasoned the stock. I cooked the fish. We bought the rings.

Allie has been wearing his ever-larger wedding bands for 65 years now, and I have been buying gefilte fish in bottles for 65 of those years. But even though I fiddled with the fish, our marriage has the ring of truth.

June 22, 1947

Would it ever come? I pestered my mother. And if it did come, what would we talk about every day from then on? I have never lived with anyone but you. How will we get along? What if . . .

My mother stopped me. "Darling. He's a wonderful man. You'll be very happy. You'll be fine. Just finish your homework and go to bed. June twenty-second will come and after that you'll be Mrs. Albert Lerman and you'll be very happy."

I wondered if she was right. Even though she was so smart about everything, her own marriage was so cold. Daddy was a nice man and I think she liked him, but she really didn't spend much time thinking about him. It was all about us, her three children; it was all about her customers and her work. She took excellent care of him in his illness. She made sure he was comfortable and cared for, very difficult in those days before health insurance. But even though I saw him reach out to her in love, I never saw her reciprocate in the same way. She was kind and good, but she clearly was not in love. I never questioned her because she was so often right, but in this situation I wasn't sure she knew what happiness meant in a marriage. But I knew she had spent every cent she had on making this a beautiful wedding, so sure was she that Albert was the right husband for me.

I took her advice and went to bed. In my dreams I feared the world would stop turning, I wouldn't be able to take a full breath, and I didn't know which I feared more – that the day would come or that the day wouldn't come. I knew I wanted to marry him, but I was so innocent about men and about the world beyond my immediate environment that I was in a panic.

It had been a long year, my last year of college. I was going into final exams and working at the local travel agency to make extra money for the wedding. I knew my mother was fast running out of money because she was planning far more lavish an event than we could afford and there was no talking her out of it. "You are marrying into a nice family," she said, "and you have to have a nice wedding."

Three rabbis married us, the retired sainted one, the current one, and the new young one, a good friend of my

father-in-law. Over one hundred guests attended. I was
resplendent in white tulle and Allie was gorgeous in his
tails, so gorgeous that he took my breath away, just as I
had dreamed.

The setting was the Louis XIV Ballroom at the Hotel
Somerset in Kenmore Square, the outstanding feature of
the hall being the stairs, which led to the balcony. The
ceremony completed, the food served, the band fading, we
changed into our travel clothes as was the custom then, and
returned to say goodbye to family and friends.

And where was my mother? At the bottom of the stairs,
having fallen from the top step in one of her excitable
moments. The finale of the wedding was a trip to the Beth
Israel Hospital where we left her with water on the knee,
smiling. "You'll be very happy, darling," she said, as I
cried my way to the car to begin our honeymoon.

Make Lemonade

It was cutting time in Brookline, the town we were
teaching in. Cutting expenses, they were giving full-time
teachers half-time jobs. The outcome was the same amount
of money for double the job. So here I was, formerly a
full-time teacher of English at junior high school level, and
they needed to cut that job to half-time. But they wanted
to keep me at full-time, so they asked, what else can you
teach? I could do a good job with social studies, I told
them. Yes, we know, they said, but we don't need that. Can
you teach computer science?

My stomach lurched. Ten years earlier, when computers became available to ordinary people, my husband, who
read the handwriting on the wall, dragged me to a computer class. You have to learn, he said; every teacher will
be expected to use computers and some will be expected to
teach them.

I was caught up in his reasoning and of course he was proven right. But I am machine-phobic. I have no idea how to fix things; I surely know how to break them.

We signed up for a class and dutifully attended for eight weeks. Just put my fingers on the keyboard, I pleaded inwardly. I can type. Maybe I'll get used to this infernal machine.

But no, in those early days the computer gurus who taught the uninitiated believed we had to know, not how to use a computer, but how one worked. We had to understand binary, digital, ones and zeros, the sort, how a computer organizes data and shuffles it into alphabetical order. I never knew how the telephone works, I screamed inwardly. Or the radio. Or electricity, or the flush on the toilet. But I have used them all and I thought that was enough.

On they droned. Ones and zeroes. Binary. The sort. Speed, accuracy, memory.

So I memorized, took the tests, did well on them because I know how to study and how to take a test. I was still totally ignorant of how to use computers, let alone how they work or how to teach them, but we soldiered on. Allie bought our first little black box, an Apple, and I word-processed to my heart's content.

He dug in with a database, spreadsheet, programming, sorting, whatever fell into his engineering mind and soul.

And so it went until the day they asked, "Can you teach computer science?"

With two children about to enter college, and the difference between half- and full-time being tuition money, I said, "Of course. English and Computer Science go together beautifully." And they did. I wrote curriculum that combined the two into an eighth-grade yearbook. They wrote, word-processed, taught me how to use graphics, and we produced a yearbook we all treasured. It got me through.

Sweet and Sour

I spent hours in the kitchen trying to recreate my mother-in-law's sweet and sour salmon. I bought large, thick salmon steaks, shiny and fresh looking, the kind I had seen her buy many times. I combined the ingredients, the canned tomatoes, the brown sugar, the fresh lemons, the onions and the raisins. I read and reread the recipe, measuring the ingredients carefully.

I cooked the salmon in the sauce, watching the mixture as it bubbled slowly, simmering. The fish was covered, but not swimming.

"Don't drown it, Ev," she had warned me many times. "Just let it poach slowly. Treat the fish with love."

I loved it and loved it, tasting as I cooked. Too sweet? More lemon. Too tart? More sugar. Not done? Keep simmering. Careful. Too well done and it's mushy. Keep watching. Don't go do something else and forget about it.

"Fish, like a child, needs love and attention," said Nana Jeanne. "And patience," she warned me.

I cooked, I watched, I tasted. I turned off the stove and let the salmon cool. Then I refrigerated it, patting it lovingly for doing a good job for me.

At mealtime I put my offering into my prettiest bowl, presenting it to my husband with a mixture of pride and trepidation.

"Nana Jeanne's sweet and sour salmon, darling," I smiled, serving him a large portion.

I watched his first bite. "Well, Ev," he said, "it's very good. Thank you, but it's not Nana Jeanne's."

Sweet and sour.

He Saved My Life

"Evelyn! Evelyn!"

I hear you, Albert. But why is your voice so strident?

So loud? I am so comfortable and happy, floating peacefully. Why are you calling me? Why does your voice sound
so desperate? Am I in danger?

"Evelyn! Evelyn! For God's sake, Evelyn, grab
the rope!"

What does he want me to do? Grab the rope. But I can't
let go of my paddle. The guide told us once we were in our
wet suits and life jackets that we should listen to his in-
structions. Paddle all the time. This is white water, you are
rafting, and you have to be alert. Don't quit no matter what
the conditions. The important thing about riding the rapids
is to keep the raft moving.

When we hit the rapids, paddle harder. In the unlikely
event that you get thrown into the water, turn over on your
back, keep your head up, hold your paddle straight up out
of the water, and float downstream. Don't forget to hold
onto that paddle.

I wondered why, but between the body suit, the life
jacket and the paddle, I felt like a knight in full body armor
and knights don't ask questions. They just do what they are
ordered to do.

"Evelyn! Evelyn! Grab the rope!"

I hear you, Albert, and holding the paddle with one
hand instead of two, I searched for the rope that must be
nearby. As my fingers found it I felt myself being dragged
against the current, floating backwards now, closer and
closer to the voice. Two strong, familiar arms pulled me
back into the raft.

"I held onto my paddle," I said, and handed it to
the guide.

Albert looked at me with a face filled with love, laughter, relief and despair. "She's unbelievable," he moaned.

When my mother picked him out for me, did she know
he would one day save my life?

The Clock

Majestic. Regal. Black, gold, mother-of-pearl inlay, white marble, black iron Roman numerals in its round face, a French provincial sweep in its black, lacquered frame, it dominates the wall above the Corian counter facing the dining area. Once it told the time on its face and struck the hour, the half hour, and repeated the hour three minutes past with its gentle, melodious chimes.

Now it is mute, both on its face and in its heartstrings. It has been wounded by a fall, disrupted by a move, and no amount of tender, loving care has been able to bring it to life again. When we returned to Brookline after a summer in Maine we found it lying on the marble coffee table, its guts spread about, its face shattered, its frame split. Apologetically, we picked up the pieces gently, carefully, not wanting to injure it further.

Al brought boxes and jars in from the garage, sorting pieces by type of wood, china face, Roman numerals, and mother-of-pearl. Each shattered piece was placed with its brethren, each identified by its look and feel. And then he went to work. He repaired each part, the beautiful exterior and the complex interior. He spent hours and days, patiently reconstructing the lovely antique French repeater clock, our centerpiece around which hung black and gold lacquered Japanese plates. Now only the plates clung to the wall as Al nursed the clock back to health. He hung it and it went back to work.

When we moved to Florida, we packed it up for our new home. The day came when he hung it on our new wall. He wound it. He set the internal pendulum so it would keep the time. For a few days it did. The delicate black metal hands moved, the hours and half hours struck. The repeater reminded us of the hour. Slowly, imperceptibly, it lost time. The chimes weakened. It got softer and softer, then quivered to a stop. The hands landed at 4:30 and the clock sighed.

Never one to seek help if he could do it himself, Al reluctantly found a professional clockmaker from France, and brought him home to examine the ailing timepiece. After many hours of standing on the counter, arms stretched over his head, the old man muttered.

"It is not willing to work," he said. "It has been wounded and it has given up." He climbed down, rubbing his tired arms and shaking his large head. "I can usually fix them," he sighed.

The clock was no better, but Al was. He smiled.

"We'll just have to love it as it is."

And so our magnificent clock guards our living room, no longer marking the time, a silent but still beautiful ornament. The Japanese plates surround it. I look at it every once in a while for the time, but it doesn't seem to mind.

Free at Last

His duffle lay on the tarmac. Dressed in khaki shorts and jacket, he paced the driveway, waiting for the van. It was still too dark to see, but perfect for spotting the headlights as they came around the corner at 4:40 a.m.

"Goodbye, my love." I kissed him and smiled.

He was headed for Tampa, Grand Junction, Colorado, Salt Lake City, Utah, Moab, Utah, and finally to the San Juan River for a seven-day canoe trip with a group of nineteen. Among the group were our son and grandson, a three-generation trip on a river snaking through the Canyon Lands.

I closed the door and made my first non-negotiated decision of the week. Should I make breakfast or go back to bed for a few hours? No one cared what I did and I was heady with the feeling. I could go back to bed for the whole day if I chose. The possibilities were endless. I could leave the bed unmade. I could stay in my pajamas all day. I could . . .

My eyes decided. They were wide-awake and not interested in more sleep at the moment. So I fixed cereal and coffee and took breakfast outside to the terrace with the morning papers. Years before, disappointed in the *Herald Tribune*, we also ordered the *New York Times* daily and Sunday. The first morning they both arrived Allie went out to get them, removed their sleeves and asked me, "Which one?"

"I'll take the *Times* first," I said, "unless you'd like it."

"No, that's OK. I'll take the *Trib* and I'll read the *Times* later."

It became our standard routine. When he finished the *Trib*, a fast read by a fast reader, he'd put down the paper and smile. I'd hand him the *Times* editorial section and go on to other parts of the paper, piling everything up for reading later in the day.

But this morning was different. Both papers were all mine. No negotiation required. Do what you want, Babe. I picked up the *Times* as usual, read the editorial page, tucked the paper away for later, dressed as usual and cleaned the house.

So much for freedom of choice.

Marriage Savers

I'm always cold. I layer my clothing, a hedge against the cold, whether I'm in air conditioning in Florida or in the woods of Maine.

My body temperature talks to me with its sense of touch. It has no wiggle room in its thermostat. The difference between too cold and just right is only a degree or two. This wouldn't be a problem for anyone else if it weren't for the fact that my dear husband is always too warm, so it became necessary early in our marriage to find "marriage savers."

It started with bedtime, with the blankets and windows. Allie liked light blankets and wide-open windows. I liked warm blankets and slightly cracked windows. All night we'd be tugging at blankets, he pushing them off and I pulling them up to my neck as we shared our king-size bed. Twin beds, we were advised. No way! I said. The best part of our marriage is the cuddling. Forget about twin beds.

We began the search for blankets: cotton, wool, polyester, and quilts, all to no avail. Nothing worked. And then we found the dual control electric blanket. The wide-open windows were no problem for me when I put my side of the blanket on five and wore turtle necks, long bottoms, gloves, socks and leg warmers. Allie, in just plain pajamas, had his blanket on zero so he was cool and I was warm. Marriage saver #1 was in place.

Then came the car comfort, especially on long trips. He liked the air conditioning on high and I liked it on low. He liked heat on low and I liked it on high. Ahah! We thought. Maybe there's a dual-control thermostat in the car. Bless the Volvo. Marriage saver #2.

And how about the house? No dual control here, but a fair compromise with the thermostat midway between his comfort level and mine, with Al wearing shorts and a tee shirt and me in long pants, a sweatshirt, and a sweater.

We'd found a way to feel good with each other.

I'll Never Share

I'm a born sharer and a born giver. As the youngest of three daughters I had to be. My two older sisters did a lot of bickering, so my role became mediator, giver, sharer, or whatever it took to make peace. It was a peculiar role for the youngest, but I think the fact that we had a working mother and a succession of assorted housekeepers meant that we had to work a lot of things out for ourselves. Since I really didn't care if I had the newest dress or the biggest piece of cake, it just came naturally to me to share and often to give away.

But the day came when I found something so special that a new feeling came over me. Ask me for anything else. Borrow at will. Take what you like. But, keep your hands and the rest of you away from my husband. He's mine and I won't share all of him, not even for a minute.

I gladly share his talents: his marvelous hands that can fix anything; his sharp mind that can burrow into the heart of the matter in a blink; his wonderful wit that can bring tears to your eyes along with your laughter; his beautiful soul that exudes love and compassion. You may share those with me, for when you do, I am ever more appreciative of the fact that he's mine. But when you go home or we go home, this man's fierce loyalty, endless caring and deep love belong to me. Call me selfish or anything else you want, but it won't matter. In spite of my mother's teaching me the value of sharing, this I won't share.

Celia, Miriam and Meyer

Family

Family is our most precious asset. We knew it as children when we missed the grandparents who never came to this country. We knew it as we grew up and mother tried so hard to keep her family together as they became estranged from one another. We know it now as we enjoy our children and their children and see them getting married and preparing to start a new family. As I reread the material in preparation for publishing this book, I am grateful for the family stories I remembered and heard, but I regret that I didn't get to interview Blossom in depth before she became so ill. Her marvelous wit and great memory would have afforded some wonderful stories.

From Generation to Generation

I see the strength of my mother's legacy in the way our children work and care about the world. I also see it in the parenting of her grandchildren, our daughter Susan and son

Bill, Mimi's daughter Phyllis and Blossom's son Robert. Each grandchild has displayed a ferocious love for his or her children: Sue for Rebecca; Bill and Martha for Lori, Bobby and Jerry; Phyllis for Garreth, Kyla and Zach; and Bobby for Lesley, Matthew and Jennie. Not only have they loved; they have nurtured, provided and encouraged their children to reach for their best and find their personal happiness.

Susan, a single parent, raised Becca under difficult circumstances. As a teacher and social worker in her early careers, she founded day care centers at her places of work so that she could be with her daughter even as she worked. She volunteered in school so that teachers could meet the needs of all the children. When she realized she wasn't making enough money to offer Becca the kind of higher education her daughter was qualified for, she went back to school nights and summers to get a Master's in Business. Once established in the business world of information technology, she encouraged Becca to go as far as she wished to go. Nana Ceil would have been proud to stand beside Sue as her great granddaughter received her LLM from Harvard Law School. We certainly were.

Bill and Martha had the joys of a great marriage and raised three wonderful children together. At their summer camp the family formed relationships with campers and counselors from all over the world. Their children may be the generation that helps to solve the conflicts between cultures.

Robert became a single parent when his children, Leslie, Matthew and Jennie, were in their teens and came to live with him. At that time he owned a delicatessen, which demanded long hours from early morning until evening. He made sure that he was home for meals, often bringing food from the deli for dinner. He supervised their education, encouraged their friends to come to his home, prepared and served holiday dinners, saw that they were all college educated and made sure his children felt safe and secure.

Phyllis didn't become a single parent until after the children were grown, but she, too, raised them under difficult economic circumstances. She used her own powerful intellect to find them the right schools and get grants and loans so Garreth, Kyla and Zach could go to college.

Ceil's "three bankbooks" raised children who honored her legacy of love and education.

The Grandfather I Never Knew

I never knew my grandfather, but I picture him. He fills a doorway with blackness, a huge brooding man in a heavy black coat that brushes the floor, a high black hat and a full black beard covering his chest. There are touches of red in his payot, the uncut sideburns which Orthodox Jews wear. His black eyes blaze with anger as he stares at me, daring me to look directly up at him. I don't. I glance up quickly, then turn aside to see his gaze directed at my four-year-old mother shivering in the corner of the one-room wooden house in the Russian shtetl where they live.

Perhaps she wants to ask him if her mother can come back to them from the hill above the house where they put her into the ground. But she is afraid to speak. One of her big brothers pushes her further into the corner with his foot.

"Stay here," he hisses. "Father is going to take his nap. Stay there and be quiet until he wakes up. Then we'll talk."

Manya

The first time I heard her name I didn't like her. I was probably three when my mother's expression "vos fer a nomen" registered. What kind of a name was Manya?

As it turned out, she really was awful, well beyond anything the name conjured up in a little girl. I thought she was disgusting, mean, ugly. She was as thin as a rail, hard boned, sharp featured with moles on her face. A witch, I thought, a witch who would eat me up and spit me out and laugh.

Whenever we went to visit my mother's older sister we'd forget how mean she was when we smelled her freshly baked, hot cinnamon buns. My sisters and I would grin at each other thinking this time it would be different. But it was always the same. Auntie would ask, "Don't the buns smell wonderful?" We'd nod, but we knew better than to ask if we could have some. Mother told us it was not polite to ask. But we could say, "Yes, delicious!" Auntie's answer, each time, "Yes, they are delicious and they are too good to eat."

But she had just begun. "Stand here in front of me," she'd order. The witch in the Gingerbread House, I'd think. The ultimate embarrassment flooded over me as she pulled up my dress to examine my underpants to see if they were clean. "Nails?" she'd command, and my sisters and I would hold out our hands for her inspection. "You never know if you will be in an accident and someone will see your dirty underpants and fingernails," she'd warn us each time. Maybe she cared about us after all, I thought, but my middle sister told me not to be so stupid. Auntie was just checking to see if our mother was doing a good job.

Her house was spotless, everything always in the same place, the house filled with delicious smells, but we were not allowed to eat, touch anything, or sit on any of the chairs. It made for a very boring visit except for the times she would show us the corsets. She had a dresser with four drawers, each crammed with the corsets she made at the

factory where she worked. Whether she stole them or they
gave them to her I don't know, but she had them, maybe
forty or fifty in all. They were gruesome with whalebones
sticking out all over them, but to a kid they were fascinating. We used to look them over with genuine interest
wondering why women wore them. Her ramrod posture
and complete lack of womanly body fat attested to the fact
that she wore one, we were sure. Of course we never asked
that or any other question. Auntie's face and manner didn't
allow for children to be heard.

We knew that Manya was ten years older than our
mother so I consoled myself that she would die soon and
we could give up our weekly visits. But irony of ironies,
she outlived her younger sister by ten years, dying at 95,
peacefully asleep in her bed. I didn't get to the house to see
her when she died but I am sure it was filled with the smell
of cinnamon buns and her bed didn't have a wrinkle in it.
She may even have died with her corset on.

Remembering My Cousin Izzy

I had to think long and hard to remember my cousin
Izzy. First I remembered how good-looking he was. He
was extremely tall, blond and handsome. He had a perfectly formed, non-Semitic nose, brilliant white teeth and
pale blue eyes with long dark eyelashes any woman would
covet. His blond hair stayed right where it belonged, lots
of it, but not too much to make him look effeminate. He
was what we used to call gorgeous.

Izzy's good looks were not lost on his mother, my aunt,
a recent immigrant from Russia. She looked over her boy
and determined that he was destined for greatness. He
would be raised as a gentleman, he would learn impeccable
table manners, he would learn how to dance and how to be
graceful with women and he would marry a lady of class,

preferably high class.

So, when the neighborhood boys were out playing football and step ball, Izzy was inside practicing the piano.

"In football you will break your hands," said Auntie. "In the piano you will find your dreams. You will become a gentleman."

As Auntie grew more Americanized, she learned that "Izzy" would never do for a Jewish boy with high aspirations, even though they were hers, not his. Fortunately, his middle name was Robert, so Izzy became I. Robert, and woe be to the person who called him Izzy.

I. Robert grew up handsome, slim, elegant, accomplished in the mannerly arts, and according to his teachers, not very bright. But he found the perfect mate, high class enough to suit Auntie, a lovely English woman who was captivated by the looks and manner of this American, so unlike the ruffians she had met on this side of the Pond.

They married and he went to work in her father's business, in the field of public relations at which he excelled. They bought a lovely country home in Long Island, had two golden-haired daughters and life moved on. We knew all about the country house because I. Robert brought pictures of it to show us when he visited.

In later years we saw very little of him and I thought about why he had been so easy to forget. Perhaps he forgot himself. When Auntie created I. Robert, I. Robert lost his Izzy.

The Setting

She stepped back to get a better view. Up close she could see only one place setting, but by stepping back she could see the whole table, twelve place settings in all.

She admired the shiny golden linen tablecloth, so carefully hand-embroidered when her fingers were still nimble enough. The matching napkins were crisp and clean, intricately folded this morning when she set the table. The sterling shone. She had finished polishing each piece over the course of three days because her arthritic fingers could only do four place settings at a time. The candles in their silver candelabra would add to the glow after they were blessed and lit for Rosh Hashanah.

Two crystal glasses sparkled at each plate, the small one filled with red wine and the larger one with water. The rays of the setting sun, slanting through the Venetian blinds, fell on the crystal, sending tiny rainbows across the table.

She smiled, satisfied. Her family would be here in just a few minutes. It was time for her to put her apron over her dress clothes, for she would personally help the maid serve each course of the dinner before she went to temple.

Jeannie nodded, complete. Everything was in its place. All would be well for another year.

Jeannie Comes of Age

She arrived by wheelchair van, smiling as the driver pushed her through the door. She acknowledged the cheers and applause of the guests at the party as if responding to an audience of opera lovers for whom she had just finished an aria. She asked the driver for her walker, and when he lowered the footrest of her chair and pushed the walker into position, she rose to her full four-feet-eleven-inches and said, "Now I can greet you."

Jeanne Lerman had arrived for her one-hundredth birth-day party. I laughed to myself as I thought, "She has come of age." But then I realized she had come of age at ninety, when her husband of nearly sixty years died.

There was no doubt that this was her day. The first-born child of Russian immigrants, Jeanne grew up in the Jewish ghetto of Boston, clothed by her father, a talented tailor. He encouraged his first born to see herself as elegant, designing and making clothes for her with fur trim and lace inserts. But she didn't have much time for elegance. Seven children followed Jeanne, who as the oldest became a surrogate mother to each. Her exhausted mother put in long days and nights trying to cope with the cooking, washing and cleaning for a family of ten.

At sixteen she graduated high school, a precocious young adult, a bookkeeper who needed a job to help her mother and father support the family. Childhood was not part of her experience. She became a woman while she was still a girl. But through it all Jeanne held herself erect, talked the Queen's English, and, when she had time, read everything she could find.

She married her boss young, raised two sons, and catered to her demanding husband until the day he died. In all those years I never knew her to express a political opinion, or to disagree with his strongly held beliefs. After his death we were breathless as we watched her emerge from his dominance. She had opinions on everything. They spilled all over us and over anyone else who listened. She talked of changes in society; she discussed politics and religion. Her years of reading flooded her conversation.

Though her eyesight was failing, she gave up large print books for regular print, using a heavy magnifying glass. "They don't put good books into large print," she commented. "They think only dummies read large print." In her assisted living facility she held court in her lounge chair, greeting the staff as they came in to see to her needs. They frequently sat on the floor at her feet so they could talk together. The young aides, often single mothers, cherished their time with her as they listened to her stories and absorbed her wisdom. She cherished her time with them as well, recognizing their difficulties in trying to make a living for their families.

Now, surrounded by family and friends, she smiled at each face as she danced by with her walker. "Much has changed," she told us, "but not love. It still makes living worthwhile."

Poor Daddy

Poor Daddy. We all said it, but I'm not sure we ever realized why we felt that way. He was sick, of course, and we knew it well. When he was home and I couldn't escape, I spent my afternoons running back and forth from the kitchen to the bedroom, bringing him hot compresses infused with herbs. My burning hands, the herbal steam choking me, my heart beating as I ran to cover his legs before the towels got cold. And then he would be so grateful for the relief that he patted me on the head, and I felt guilty for being resentful. I so wanted to be at my friend Ellie's house being a kid, instead of being here with him, being a nurse.

But what did we know of his emotional state? He was confined to bed, to the hospital, or exiled to Florida or Arizona where, he hoped, he would feel better. He had no say in family decisions because he was not the breadwinner, and in those days men didn't do subordinate things like help their wives. That wasn't their role. In another era he might have been the bookkeeper for Mother's dressmaking business. He might have found a low ironing board so he could sit down and press the finished garments. He would have made out the tickets, collected the money, but then men had to be in charge. And if not in charge, then they were out of sight. How helpless, how hopeless he must have felt. How useless.

And did we respect his thinking? We knew he was

a serious reader and a thinker. He was a Socialist who understood politics, who felt that government should help people who needed it. But we ignored his thinking because Mother was a Czarina. She loved everything beautiful, upper class, out of reach. Her upbeat manner, her optimism, her breathtaking energy and love captivated me, while our daddy depressed me.

Now I understand. I feel his arthritic pain in my hips and my hands and am grateful when the physical therapist relieves it. I react to Daddy's feelings of uselessness when I understand that the Women's Liberation movement allowed men to be nontraditional, to fill roles never before available to them. Most of all, I can relate to his politics. He made me a Democrat, a liberal, even though my heart danced to my mother's aristocratic tune. He even, much to my surprise, made her a Democrat as we all sat around the kitchen table and listened to FDR's Fireside Chats. She was hooked, not by the president's policies, but by his aristocratic English. She loved the WASP and the Harvard in him, and forgot about the politics.

I am happy that in my old age I can relate to my father, understand him, respect him, and love him. He was a fine man at the wrong time in history. I am sorry he's not here for me to tell him.

Father Speaks

I picture my father on a good day, standing at the ironing board, my mother at her machine, nine-year-old me in my usual chair watching her work, and my beautiful, blonde sixteen-year-old sister coming into the sewing room.

"Mother, I need to talk to you," said she. My mother stopped her work, surprising me, for when she and I talked she worked all the time. Why did she stop, I wondered.

Perhaps she heard the urgency in my sister's voice or perhaps she remembered Miriam telling her that she never listened.

"Yes, darling. I am listening."

"I want to take dancing lessons."

My mother didn't get a chance to answer, for my usually quiet father slammed down the iron onto the ironing board, limped over to where Miriam stood, lifted her chin with his hand, and talked right into her eyes.

"You will not take dancing lessons. You will not become a dancer. Dancers are 'courevehs'; they take men to their rooms for money, they smoke, they drink, they wear makeup. Dancing leads to all these things. You will not dance!"

He dropped his hands, turned, limped out of the room to his bedroom, leaving all of us shocked by his outburst.

We turned to our mother for an explanation. Usually smiling and full of talk, she sat mute and embarrassed. "I don't want to talk about it. He's thinking of the bad women in Russia and he is afraid for you. You cannot take dancing lessons."

This was my first lesson in sex education, even though I didn't really understand it. My sister and I were shocked, not only by my father's outburst, but also by my mother's response. She almost never backed him up, often granting us anything we wanted and not telling him. We knew the game. But not this time. I had no idea what any of it meant, only that you couldn't discuss it and it was bad.

My father had finally spoken.

The Road Not Taken

Suppose she had become the dancer she always wanted to be. Her life might have been entirely different. She might have married a different man, been a different person. She was light on her feet, had a fine sense of rhythm, and was a five-foot-five blonde with seductive blue eyes.

Maybe that was the problem. When our father, Meyer, looked at my oldest sister all he saw was the women of his youth who haunted the corner of the street he lived on.

--Don't go near them, warned his mother, they will ruin you. Normally soft spoken, she shouted at him every time he went out to find his friend Yossel.

--They are bad women. They dance and they smoke and they look for young boys to ruin.

Meyer was intrigued and terrified at the same time. The women in his family, his mother and his three sisters, didn't dance, didn't smoke, and as far as he knew, didn't ruin young boys. What could that mean? The only "ruin" he knew was a house next door that people called "the ruin." The windows were broken, the porch was splintered, and the bricks were loose.

Would a ruined boy be broken like that? Would his teeth be loose, his bones broken, his arms shattered? Why would those women do that to him? But he didn't dare to ask because he knew his mother would be angry with him for talking back.

Now he had a daughter growing up in America. She was blonde like those women, and she wanted to dance. The times were different, he knew, and he was living in a new country. In the old country everything was forbidden unless the Rabbi said it was all right.

You drank only to celebrate the Sabbath, and then you drank sparingly. A drunk Jew was a "shandeh," a shame for his family. And women didn't smoke, ever. Dancing was allowed only at a wedding, and then you could dance only with members of the same sex. Nice women didn't become dancers.

Here it was different. He could tell by what he heard on
the radio, what he saw once a week in the motion pictures,
and what he read in the papers. But mostly he was learning
about the new customs from this American daughter of his
who spoke to him in English.

 "Women do dance here, Daddy," she told him, "and
they smoke, too. That doesn't make them bad women. I
really want to become a dancer."

He tried; he really tried. He wanted her eyes to sparkle
the way they did when Civia allowed her to do things she
said all the other girls did. And he wanted her to hug and
kiss him when she thanked him for permission to dance.
But he couldn't. The bad women were too ingrained in his
mind. I can't allow my daughter to become a loose woman,
he told himself, and sighed.

To her he said, "No, daughter, I am sorry. I can't allow
it," and he buried his head in the newspaper.

Mimi ran to her room. She hummed to herself in front
of the mirror, swaying her body to the rhythm of "Night
and Day," dancing with an imaginary Fred Astaire, swing-
ing her hair like Ginger Rogers. But the tears streaming
down her face brought her back to reality. I'll never be
allowed to dance, she told the mirror. I'll have to become a
secretary or a home economics teacher, even in America.

Her body stiffened, her eyes lost their sparkle; she
shook off Fred, and put on her apron to make dinner.

Excerpts from Susan's E-mails
When She Was Working in Israel
February 22, 2005

This is an amazing experience. Going to Jerusalem was
unbelievable! Here is a picture of the Wailing Wall with
the Golden Dome above it. Only Muslims can go to the
Temple Mount. I went to the female side of the Wall and

prayed and left my note in the Wall. I could hardly breathe when I walked away.

February 26, 2005

As you have probably read or seen, a suicide bomber blew himself up at a popular nightclub last night. Just to let you know, our group does not live close to that club and we are all okay.

April 9, 2005

Every day of this adventure is something new. I am now in Ashkelon.

This is clearly NOT Tel Aviv. Ashkelon is a very old city that is in the process of transformation. There are very old, very small homes and mostly old apartment complexes in the heart of the city.

But then there is the shore and folks with money have discovered this is very nice scenery. And then there is Bernea, another coastal community of Ashkelon, which is becoming very posh. Add to that the resettlement of Gaza and it gets very interesting.

The state of Israel is giving each family that is being re-settled 250-500K plus land to move where? To the North-ern corner of Ashkelon. Now we mix in the population, mostly immigrants from Russia and Ethiopia. There is very little English in the shops and on the streets. This weekend I am here alone as everyone else is visiting elsewhere and Israelis stay home on the Sabbath.

Getting food is a challenge because it is the Sabbath and the restaurants (all two of them) are closed. I go to the corner store and find what I think is tuna, but turns out to be mystery meat. So I am living on pasta, eggs, cereal and bread and butter this weekend.

Oh, I forgot. I did find some wonderful white raisins

and some oranges. There is, however, a fabulous view from this apartment – the sea, the marina and the beach. So all is not lost.

April 11, 2005

Update! Things are much better today. Good day at the office and I found a big grocery store. At first I bought only what I knew, and then I met a Russian woman behind the dairy counter. In my Hebrew School Hebrew I told her that my imah had a Russian mother from the Ukraine, so I was of Russian descent. She was so pleased that she decided I needed some help. When she called the front desk and asked for assistance in English, three young Israeli soldiers came to my rescue.

They thought it was something else to be helping an American. Once I got the hang of what was in the dairy case the Russian lady took over. I pointed and she said "good" or "not so good."

After trial and error and lots of tasting of cheeses, herring and the finest smoked sable, I bought and bought. I had the most wonderful fresh salad with the sable, a fresh dark rye roll and dill cream cheese. Tomorrow I'm off to Tel Aviv for a meeting at the office, followed by a trip to the U.S. Embassy. I'm driving by myself and hopefully this time I won't get lost and have to call Yuli for directions and guidance to my destination.

Love to all,
Susan

Excerpts from Becca's E-mails
When She Was Working in Afghanistan
March 30, 2007

First may I wish you all a happy 1386. We have just had our solar New Year here, called Naw Ruz (new day in

Dari/Persian). I can't figure out what happened here 1386 years ago, but I do know that the calendar started on the day of the vernal equinox as determined by astronomical observations in Kabul and Tehran, and was March 21. Afghanistan basically shuts down on Naw Ruz for one very long weekend, which we chose to fill together with quality man and feline time. The weather is beautiful here in Herat, warm and breezy, not cold or hot. Even in Kabul I hear the weather is improving. Spring has definitely sprung and everything is in bloom. I love it. The gardener came to our compound today and pulled up all the carrots that survived the winter. Apparently, eating carrots after Naw Ruz is simply not done. I've been doing some gardening of my own, filled my little apartment with new plants and trees and viney things. I even got myself a little orange tree.

OK, for the business report. My job has changed a bit. I am still employed by the NRC but in a somewhat different capacity. Previously I was managing two of the NRC's information counseling and legal assistance programs in Afghanistan, the Herat office and the Supreme Court team. The Court has now been streamlined a bit and will be merged into two Kabul legal aid centers so I will hand that over to my colleague Sarah. I will still be managing the Herat office and will be working with those in need of assistance to build their own houses rather than those with disputes over property they "own."

The new part of my job is technical advisor to a research project being run by AREU, a very well respected research- and writing-oriented organization that focuses largely on rural land issue conflicts. I will be responsible for running the operations, doing some report writing, developing teaching materials and conducting a training program for legal professionals and government officials on methods involved in dispute resolution. Feels a bit over-whelming, but it's a great challenge.

My health is good, not a single parasitic amoebic cystic thing of any kind and I found a real live yoga instructor in Herat with a studio and a class. Amazing.

So life is good. I love you and miss you.

Becca

Connections

"We're family," my daughter-in-law answers me when I ask her if something would be too much for her to do. "Of course not," she says, "we're family."

I wonder if my son Bill married Martha because she reminded him of his grandmother Ceil. She has the same shapely legs, the love of food in huge quantities, unstint-ing love for her family, and a personality that makes everyone smile.

How did Martha and I make our connection? With your own children you grow with the connection, but with a newcomer full grown? And from Kankakee, Illinois? Where is it, for God's sake? My son says he married a Central American. But here she is, a central part of our lives, the mother of three of our wonderful grandchildren and we're connected. Is it the marriage vow, the mother role? Perhaps, but there is more.

There's a piece of humanity in Martha, an understand-ing of others, of the person she's involved with, an invis-ible thread that reaches out and surrounds you with a close-ness of understanding, a cord of insight, a connection.

The Bosses' Daughter
Lori Lerman (College Essay) 11/01/01

I was six years old when I realized that I did not belong at Camp Caribou. I loved it, but I had to leave. The camp had been in my family since my grandparents bought it in 1968. It is in central Maine nestled on a lush, 200-acre peninsula. My parents took over in 1983. It is a child's dream, and it was mine, as well. Unfortunately for me, it is a boys' camp.

It was not until ten years later, after attending a girls' camp during my summers, I returned to Camp Caribou as a tennis counselor. It meant a great deal to me to succeed. Running the camp was not only how my parents made a living, but also the center of our family's world, and one I had been somewhat left out of. I wanted to fit in with the other counselors, but I was the bosses' daughter, and the only female counselor. I earned their trust and respect by working hard, not expecting that I would be treated any different, and always doing more than what was asked of me. They finally stopped beginning our conversations with "Don't tell this to your dad, but . . ."

I love kids, especially young ones, and love working with them, playing with them, and teaching them. As it turned out, the most important things I learned were off the court. I became a mother figure for the youngest campers, a sister and a friend to the older ones. Boys trusted me with problems that they felt they could not share with male counselors, for fear of being made fun of.

Taylor H. was only seven years old, and this past summer was his first time at camp. He was always on my court for instructional periods, but our friendship developed outside of tennis. Taylor was very homesick and he never liked to cry in front of his bunkmates or counselors. At night, I sometimes talked to him about his dog, and other things he missed from home. Taylor turned out to be an excellent camper, making many contributions to the camp, and enjoying his first summer away.

I had changed this summer, going from outsider in my

own summer home, to someone who was a trusted and respected member of the camp community. I finally earned a place in this central aspect of my family's life, something very important to me. But, of equal importance, I learned that by working hard, you gain trust and respect; and by listening to other people's problems, you not only help them to succeed, but you succeed yourself. These skills are very important when applying oneself to any new environment, even college. The things that I learned at camp will stay with me forever and I will be able to use what I learned for the rest of my life.

. . . Ten years later, I'm proud to say that I'm now working full-time with our family's business. So much has happened since I wrote this college essay, and although I was only seventeen then, many of the themes still ring true today. The things you learn at camp will always stay with you.

A College Reference for Bobby

To whom it may concern
From Evelyn Lerman
Re Robert I. Lerman
August 14, 2004

As they say on TV, "for the record," I am Bobby Lerman's grandmother. That may make it difficult for you to believe the legitimacy of my assessment of Bobby's strengths. But I will try to be objective, using all my non-grandmotherly skills of teaching and evaluating, gathered in thirty-plus years of careers in education.

It has been our privilege, my husband's and mine, to watch Bobby grow through all the summers of his life, because we have all lived together at the family summer camp for boys. Our earliest memories are of him as an infant, playing on a blanket on our screened porch. Our latest observations are of this summer when Bobby was a counselor aide at camp.

In between we observed him as a young boy, too young to live in a cabin with summer campers, then as a camper, and finally as staff-in-training in his favorite area, basketball. In all of these roles, Bobby handled himself with grace, integrity, modesty, and dignity.

To be the son of the camp directors is not an easy role. The other boys and the staff are always watching. If you behave too well, you're a nerd. If you behave too badly, you're a showoff who thinks he can get away with anything because his parents are the directors. Finding a middle road in which you can be one of the boys, trusted and valued, is the finest line to walk, especially for a youngster who doesn't know the rules for such a complicated dance.

But Bobby got it intuitively, from the days when he was too young to play but stood on the sidelines and cheered the boys on to the days in which he played his hardest with the teams and as an individual, up to the present time when, in his beloved basketball court, he guides young boys on their way to becoming men.

Bobby's innate common sense combines with his solid knowledge of other people's feelings to make him a joy to be with. He never pulls rank, he never oversteps, yet he's always part of what he is doing. My family, including his sibs, tease me about thinking Bobby is perfect. "Oh, don't ask Grandma about Bobby! She thinks he's perfect."

They made me think about why I do think so highly of Bobby, and it has come to me over the years. Bobby is a peacemaker, a good sport, a supporter of others' strengths and a defender of others' weaknesses. He is involved in keeping himself healthy and strong, but he doesn't judge or criticize others who don't share those values. He follows his own judgment, not going along with the group if it isn't something he chooses to do, but not making the group feel that he is doing a better thing. He is respected by his peers for his independent mind, and liked by them for his warm spirit and endless support.

I strongly recommend Bobby to a school that is looking for an athletic, independent, motivated student who will bring his many personal and interpersonal skills to a campus. He will be liked, respected, valued, and enjoyed as a friend, a colleague, and a contributor.

E-Mail from Jerry

Jerry had just completed high school and was in Tanzania on a summer program.

From: Jerry Lerman <jerryblitzlerman@gmail.com>
Date: Tue, Jul 3, 2012 at 6:53 AM
Subject: Re: here (Tanzania, East Africa)
To: Camp Caribou <info@campcaribou.com>

Hi mama! The smells and sounds are like nothing I have ever heard before. I am two minutes away from the beach, the Indian Ocean, which is aqua blue with warm water. Today all of us are going there to hang out and do some swimming. In a couple of days I'm going to a crocodile farm so you should let Bobby and Alex know that. I had my first day of work today and I loved it. I have my own class of twenty nine- and ten-year-old kids who already have taken a liking to me. They are all extremely cute and awesome to be around. I have pictures of my class and everything around me. I was nervous at first standing in front of a classroom full of kids but I got into it quickly. It is an English medium school so all subjects are taught in English as well as Swahili. I played outside with them today and taught them how to tell time and some world history. All the little kids refer to me as Sir Jerry because it is polite according to their culture. This might be one of

the longest emails I have ever written in my career. I love
all you guys a ton and miss all of you.

Peace, Jigz

P.S. I am emailing from a local Internet cafe.

The Heritage

She was meticulous about her weight, her clothes, her
hair. And her taste was exquisite. So when she reached
for the silver piece on the top shelf in the antique shop on
Charles Street, I paid attention.

"What is it?"

"It's an antique egg holder. The English gentry used
them at breakfast to serve soft-boiled eggs on their buffet
sideboards."

I marveled at her eye, the way she spotted lovely things
in the midst of so much that was ordinary. She knew what
was beautiful and collectible.

"But why would you want one?"

"Not for me, for you. I already have one. One day
you'll use it to serve hard-boiled eggs at the Seder."

I gasped. "My Seder? You know our mother-in-law will
do them forever."

"Nobody's forever. So buy it for her."

I looked at my chic sister-in-law, dressed for shopping
as if she were going to meet someone at the Ritz for lunch.
I knew my mother-in-law preferred her company to mine
when they shopped and went to lunch together. That was
fine with me because I really didn't enjoy the shopping and
went along reluctantly. After a while I noticed they seemed
happier when I said, "No, thanks."

So this was an opportunity for me to do something nice
for my mother-in-law. It was a great gift; Mother used it
every Passover for all the years she did the Seder.

Our lives moved on. We had deaths and other losses,

but my mother-in-law lived to a beautiful 101. When we cleaned up her house we found the egg holder, pitted and tarnished from many years in Florida. It was so beautiful still that we had it resilvered and polished.

Each year I take it out of its zippered cover, ask Allie to give it a quick polish, and we fill it with hard-boiled eggs for the Seder and remember. I think of my sister-in-law and her exquisite taste. I remember Jeannie's elegant Seders. I remember our grown children as little ones at her table. I remember our heritage, all reflected in the beautiful egg holder.

Looking Back at Shadows

My family is gone but its shadows are still here. I see my oldest sister telling me to pull up my socks and stop eating so much. I see her trying to grow into womanhood and having no opportunity to be a child.

Then I spot my middle sister competing with me for every prize, every commendation, and any words of praise floating in our world. I realize again that she is smarter, quicker, sharper, funnier, a better cook and more popular. She's a glimmer, like the signal on the dashboard that reminds the driver that the car needs maintenance. With all her superior talents, she is still competing with me for who's better.

I see my father, who was a shadow in my life, but is no longer so vaguely defined. I see him sick and quiet, but a thoughtful intellectual, a reader nursing his illness in the bedroom, a man in a world where he can't make a living. His ideas float in the hallway and into the kitchen where we talked the politics of the Nazis and of the world that let the rich get richer and the poor get poorer. He comes closer into view as I recall his deep thinking and commentary.

And I see a snap of my mother, the mother who raised

me to be president, but who would have been happy with my being a professor, a judge, a doctor or a teacher. Girls could be anything, do anything, she said, but it was also important to be happy. Find your muse was her message. Life is glorious and huge. Swallow it whole, then chew. In spite of a domineering father and no mother, she brushed off the behavior of her brothers and sister and found her own values to live by. She is there, enveloping me still. Light and lovely, strong and heroic, warm and comforting – she is there.

Part Three

About Me

My Friend Ellie

Mother moved us from Jamaica Plain to Brookline when I was entering sixth grade. There is probably no more needy time in the life of a young girl. She is growing and growing up, changing both physically and emotionally and terrified of being left out of a group.

I needed a friend.

Finding Ellie

Growing up in Brookline, Massachusetts was bitter sweet. It was sweet to be in a junior high that was exciting and vibrant, to be surrounded by students who were attractive and smart. But it was bitter to be a come-lately outsider with the wrong clothes and the wrong stories to tell. They all shared, or so it seemed to me, memories of elementary school, neighborhood parties, lost loves and found loves, and even the simple things like going to the movies together.

I was an immigrant from the town next door and my

memories were of going to St. Mary's Church with my Catholic friends, dipping my fingers into holy water, and hoping my Jewish God wouldn't smite me. Those were not sharable stories with my new Jewish classmates so I mostly kept quiet and listened, longing for a real friend.

And one day, there she was – a tall, beautiful, blonde girl, as big as I was, with a gorgeous smile and a welcoming hug. She adopted me and took me home to her warm, distinguished Yankee mother, a woman of grace and elegance, as poor as we were, and most important, a mother who was home after school.

So I no more went home after school to our quiet, dark apartment where my two older sisters expected me to be as unhappy as they were. Instead I went to Ellie's house where Mae had sandwiches without crusts and chocolate frappes whipped up in a large covered bottle with an eggbeater in it. It turned milk and Morgan's chocolate ice cream into magic. As we ate, they came: Margie, Ellie's older sister who played the piano, Dave, the trumpeter, Joe the drummer and Mike the clarinetist. Ellie added her beautiful soprano to the quintet and I sat tingling with excitement over the music of Benny Goodman and Tommy Dorsey. The afternoons flew by, and I left reluctantly to help with supper and the care of our sick father.

I timed my arrival so that I would be saved from the wrath of my sisters by the arrival of my mother returning from work. They glared, but they didn't attack when mother was there. The afternoon glow of the glorious music and the rich food, the intimacy of the friendships and the warmth of the home carried me through the evening. By then our home seemed inviting, too, because wherever my mother was there was comfort.

Memories of afternoons at Ellie's still come wherever there is joy, music, laughter, friendship, and love. They

may be clouded over at times by life, but they are never
lost. A Benny Goodman theme, a Tommy Dorsey rhythm,
and I am back at Ellie's, sipping on Mae's magic frappes,
savoring the expansive glow of friendship.

Smoke and Mirrors

We were young. We were gorgeous. Ellie and I rode our
bikes and sang like Bonita Granville as she rode through
the Swiss Alps. Our hair flew behind us. We stood on
the pedals so we looked like models or, at the very least,
like bike riders in competition. We were heading for
Norumbega, the dance hall on the Charles River.

It was a fantasyland in Newton, Massachusetts, with
paddleboats and ducks on the outside and as many teenagers as could fit or had money enough to go dancing
in that hallowed place. Glen Miller and Tommy Dorsey
brought their bands, and we knew every word of the songs
they played for the dancers. We wished for a date to take us
there, hoping to get lucky with one of the few guys around
just before they were drafted.

The magic night came. I don't remember the boy, but
I do remember the hall. It was a huge wooden dance floor
in which dark royal red velvet curtains kept out any light
so that the glistening ball in the middle of the ceiling could
throw its glitter over the dancers. The ball also illuminated
the brown velvet couches where dancers "made out"
between numbers, while the smoke from five hundred
cigarettes clouded the room.

Smoke permeated everything. I danced, kissed my date
as I balanced a cigarette on the arm of the chair and inhaled
deeply, pretending I was in the arms of Paul Henreid in
"Now Voyager." Paul had just lit my cigarette in his mouth
and handed it to me. I was in love with Hollywood, in love
with the movies, in love with the music, in love with men

and in love with love.

The ballroom was endless. It went on and on for miles, it seemed, and yet we never went anywhere on the dance floor. So great was the crush of bodies when the big bands played that we were stuck in a five-foot square and spent the evening in that spot for song after song. I suggested to my date that we leave the crush and head for the other room.

He laughed and I blushed. What's funny? He eased me out of the traffic and danced me straight ahead. "Reach out," he said.

I jumped back as my hand touched the mirror. He grinned and danced me sideways.

"Reach out," he said. I tried again, confronting myself.

"I get it. I get it." I tried to smile through my tears of embarrassment, all my sophistication melted away in the smoky mirror.

Another Mother, Maebelle

1862 Beacon Street was just a red brick three-story apartment house, but one of those apartments was my special home away from home during the years I grew from an adolescent thirteen to a grownup eighteen. This story is about Mae Elva Arnold, about her kitchen and about her love.

Ellie Arnold was my true and only best friend at elementary school, and it was to her home she brought me after school, an escape from my home with an absent mother and a sick father, an escape to a home filled with a mother, food, music, friendship and love.

Mae's kitchen was a relatively small room, perhaps ten by ten, with a black stove and stovepipe, glassed-in cabinets, a wooden table in the middle, and six colonial chairs covered with tufted calico cushions tied to the rungs of the backs. A blue and pink linoleum cloth covered the table, easily wiped up after meals.

The counters held miracles, according to my untutored eye, miracles with which Mae turned out meals I knew nothing of. No huge melons here, no uncut challahs, no roasted chickens dripping on the plate, nothing familiar from my Jewish home where my mother never cooked, but filled our table with food she could buy ready-to-eat.

But Mae, a Yankee New Englander, New Hampshire born and bred, was a cook, a pickler, a preserver; she treasured all the fruits of the earth and saved them before they were "gone by," such that crusts of white bread, cut off from sandwiches, became bread pudding, roast lamb became minced lamb on toast, and ice cream, stored in the single ice cube tray in the freezer, became a frappe under her talented eggbeater jar.

The eggbeater fit into its own jar, with a cover, no doubt the first blender to be made. Beside it, the meat grinder clamped onto the counter so that the cook could fill it and turn the handle to pulverize the meat, the onions, and the spices. Sugar from a blue and white covered sugar bowl, unheard of in my house where we used salt and pepper only, was served with hot oatmeal accompanied by brown sugar, maple syrup and heavy cream.

All of these wonders greeted me after school or on weekends when Ellie and I spent every moment we could together. Mae's kitchen was mine through her unstinting love for Ellie and her friends. The food never really became mine, but the memories did. I learned from Mae that, coming at life from a whole different perspective, strength can be in soft-spoken acts of kindness as well as in large flourishing acts of courage.

Ev and Al at Camp Caribou, 1968.

All Work and No Play

When I came home from school and Daddy was there, he'd always ask if I had homework. If I did, he'd say, "First you work and then you play." It was the mantra he learned in the old country where play was unheard of, since survival depended on work alone. So I grew up watching my mother work and hearing my father expressing his opinion about work. Work was not a chore; work was a value.

Working

Working has always been as natural for me as breathing. My first recollections of my mother are of her energy as she hurried to get dressed to go to work. One particularly cold winter morning she kissed me goodbye while it was still dark and told me to stay in bed until the house got warmer. She was on her way to light the stove in the

cleaning/dyeing/tailor shop she owned with my father.
Once the stove was warm, my father would join her there a
few hours later. By then she would have finished the tailoring of the men's suits and have them ready for Daddy
to press.

The front room of the store, the part the customers
came into, would remain dark until Daddy arrived because
the customers should never see Mother as she worked on
men's clothes. Tailors were men then, in the 1930's, and
dressmakers were women. Mother would be working on a
man's jacket or pants, which the day before Daddy would
have appeared to be marking for alterations. He would
stand behind the customer, a tape measure draped around
his shoulders over his vest, while Mother, standing in the
doorway between the two rooms of the store, would have
eyeballed the measurements for the alteration. Daddy was
not a tailor, but a dyer of fabrics and a presser. Even then,
only in his thirties, he was suffering the pain of crippling
arthritis and debilitating asthma, illness contracted in the
steppes of Siberia, while fighting as a conscript in the Army
of Czar Nicholas II.

But he pressed what he could, and Mother sewed from
early morning 'til late at night. Together they made enough
money to keep the three of us, my two sisters and me, in
food, clothing, and shelter. By the time Mother got home
at night we were all asleep, so the next time I would see
her would be in the dark of early morning, unless I stopped
for a hug on my way to elementary school or unless it was
Sunday, the only day they both stayed at home.

When Daddy succumbed to his arthritis and asthma and
began spending his days in the darkened bedroom down
the hall of our apartment, we had survived the Depression,
the store was long gone, and Mother worked from the front
room of the apartment we lived in. Her hours were just as

long, but she was at home, the forerunner of today's working alternative. By this time I was in high school, and I was working at the local Touraine store on weekends.

These were the days when Mother and I sat together and had our long talks, she working at her sewing machine. The notion of her sitting still without something to do was not possible. I carry this with me to this day, for if I find myself in a chair now, not reading or writing, I end up biting my nails, just to be busy doing something.

As a young married woman with two small children I was busy enough caring for them, the household, and my husband's needs. But I had graduated college, I had been trained and programmed to work, and I had time on my hands, as our two children grew older. Sue was a freshman in high school and Bill in the sixth grade when I realized that one more day of women's organization meetings, one more ad book, one more luncheon, one more PTA meeting, and I would be needing psychiatric attention. What a waste of money that would be, I thought. Better to spend it on something productive, something that could be turned to a profit. I hunted around and was caught up one day by an article in the newspaper inviting graduates to the Boston Simmons Club meeting. A meeting yes, but maybe it would lead to something.

The speaker was from Harvard, talking about a master's degree for women. Plan M they called it. M for Mother? Mature? Matronly? No one really knew, but it was at the School of Education, and I decided I would become a teacher. My first training as a journalist was useful. I had published a trade journal for the family business for ten years and I had used my skills in all kinds of organizational work. But it was time for a new career. Since I enjoyed working with kids in Scouting, loved being with my own kids, and devoured learning, why not teach?

Three part-time years later, balancing home and school, I graduated with a Master's degree in Education and was hired to teach in my hometown of Brookline, Massachusetts. I tell you all these things just to let you know that I was now, finally, at the age of forty, a real workingwoman. Paid, however modestly in those years, a member of a Union, a hurry-up-and-get dressed to go to work mother, a bearer of a paycheck each week. I could now ignore housework without guilt, we could eat out at a moment's notice, and the laundry could iron the shirts. I could watch TV when time permitted without feeling the need to be busy, since I was plenty busy all day long. I had found myself in the world of work and no matter how hassled or frantic, how torn up by the need to be a good wife and mother as well as a good teacher, I felt fulfilled and happy. From that time to this I have worked at multiple careers: teacher of grades three through eight, specialist as teacher of Language Arts, teacher of Social Studies, Director of English, Supervisor of English, Vice Principal, computer teacher, Personnel Director and mediator.

Concurrent with all these careers in education, my husband and I bought a resident boys' camp in Maine, which we owned and directed for fifteen years. Through work I found much fulfillment; for fulfillment I sought work. As each career ended it was time to let it go, retrain, refuel and begin again. Each ending was a beginning. My husband and I both retired from teaching and from camp directing, moved to Florida from Massachusetts, and in this new setting I am once again finding fulfillment in teaching and writing. Work is a necessary part of my life.

My mother used to say, "When people tell me they have time on their hands or say they need to kill some time, I don't understand. There is never enough time for all the work that has to be done."

Student Teaching

"Red Reading Group, rise! Red Reading Group, go to Reading Corner."

I followed the third graders, five boys and three girls, to the Reading Corner, all of us dutifully carrying our readers. I sat there, uncomfortable, squeezed into a child's seat in the circle. The children seemed even less comfortable, at rigid attention waiting for Miss Dandridge to join the group. The tension was electric.

Who would be called on to read? Who would stumble? Who would be yelled at? Who wasn't prepared? I was as tense as they were, for when Miss Dandridge humiliated one of them, I felt humiliated, too.

"Red Reading Group, open your books to chapter three, page twelve."

We all obeyed except for bright-eyed Jesse whose curly-haired head was buried in the book. So engrossed was she in the story that she didn't hear the order, and we waited for the axe to fall.

"Jesse, you are reading ahead. You know that's not permitted. You will sit with your book closed and your hands folded during Reading Group."

Jesse flushed, her eyes brimming with tears as she closed her book and folded her hands. I reached over to comfort her.

"Mrs. Lerman, the blackboard requires washing. During reading group you will wash the board. The last time you left it streaky. See to it that this time it is done properly."

I winked at Jesse surreptitiously, signaling her that I was being punished, too, but we would both live through it. As I washed and listened, I reviewed the two years of graduate school education I was completing with this internship. In June I would receive my Master's in Education and would be teaching full-time.

I reviewed the courses in philosophy, in cognitive and affective learning, in methodology, in psychology. I had learned a lot, much of it useful, some of it questionable. I laughed to myself as I considered where I had learned the most. Right here, I thought. Right in this classroom observing a Vermont woodshed-personality spinster teaching third graders. It was the perfect setting in which to develop my style. Whatever Miss Dandridge did, I would never do. Whatever she said, I would never say. I would be the positive to her negative. I would be the other side of her coin. I would become a teacher.

Team Teaching

She was beautiful, I thought. Not only beautiful, but young, elegant, confident, and sexy. I was forty-five, perhaps twenty years older than she. We were teaching partners, sharing the same eighth graders. When I was honest with myself I acknowledged that I was intimidated by her.

How could this be? I am the mature one here. I've been teaching for five years. Why am I overwhelmed by this young woman? What's wrong? It was the early seventies, the end of the sixties, when the world had turned upside down. All the old rules were out and the new rules weren't settled in yet. It was the era of feminism, a time when women were demanding equal rights, a time when women and men, too, were redefining their roles at work, in society and at home. It was the era when my husband, who had always opened doors for me and carried my bundles, drew up to a mailbox and said with a twinkle in his eye, "ERA, Ev, you get out and mail the letters. ERA stands for Evelyn's Reduced Advantages."

"She wants it both ways," he said of my colleague. "She wants to be seductive and at the same time she wants

to be a feminist, with no emphasis on her sexuality or that
of other females. I'm not playing her game!"

I wished I could be as sure of my reactions as he was.
But I didn't know what my feelings were. She was introducing a bold new curriculum, one that was to become a
model for school systems all over the country. She was
good at her work and I was impressed. At the same time I
didn't like her manipulative ways, not only with male colleagues but with women as well. She taught moral development, but her personal morality extended only as far as
it benefited her. If not, no holds were barred in her quest
for success and prominence in her field.

And I was the poor stepsister. When the students we
both taught needed supplies, she sent them to me. When
they needed help of any kind, when they needed watching or monitoring, she sent them to me. Otherwise, when
it was standup, showoff teaching time, she was the leader,
the illustrious teacher of the eighth grade.

Cinderella cleaned the hearth; Judith went to the Ball.
Bedazzled as I was by her glamorous feminism, I went
along as her partner. But even a Cinderella can get tired of
being on her knees surrounded by ashes. One day the class
came to me for their English lesson, having just left her
class. They were distracted. I couldn't get their attention,
couldn't teach, couldn't engage them at all.

"What's up?" I asked them.

They had been watching a wartime film, they told me.
They were despondent, unbelieving. How could man be
so cruel to man? How could he be so inhuman? We talked.
We talked some more. We processed the film, the times,
their feelings. We had a powerful discussion for the hour
and they left feeling a little better.

I was furious. How dare she set me up like that? Not a
word beforehand, not a collegial discussion of the needs of

her curriculum, let alone the needs of mine. School ended and I sought her out, still fuming. "Do your own dirty work from now on," I told her. "Get your own supplies. Keep your own Band-Aids handy.

"And let me know when the kids are going to be exposed to overwhelming material. I might even surprise you by becoming a real partner. I'm a good teacher and, moreover, I have twenty years of maturity on you. You might be surprised at what I could contribute. We could be a real team."

I knew what I felt and I told her. And I felt good.

Teaching

He stood at my desk, a fourth grader clutching his paper to his chest. His head barely reached to the top of the desk, but his hair caught my eye. It was combed carefully, brown and shiny, with a stubborn cowlick shooting up from the end of the part. I could picture his mother working on it with spit and water, but the cowlick held its own.

"Mikey," I said, putting what I thought was a smile into my voice. "What's wrong? Why are you clutching your paper to your chest?"

Mikey didn't answer.

"Mikey, why are you here at my desk? I didn't call you up."

"I know you like us to share our work with you when we're done and if we don't come up you'll call us anyway," he mumbled.

"But, Mikey, I don't want you to be unhappy. What are you afraid of?"

He finally looked up at me. "Well," he said, "I don't like to show you my paper because it's perfect until you read it."

My mother's teaching was confirmed. "By meer bist du

Al – ready to play after we retire.

schein." To me you are beautiful, she said, no matter what I had done. That's what the kids needed to feel. That's the day I learned how to teach.

Time to retire.

Section Ten

All Play and No Work?

On a snowy day in December of 1992, Allie and I brushed off the car and headed for Sarasota, Florida, and our retirement. We had retired first from camping, then from teaching, and we were ready to spend the rest of our lives together in a warm and relaxed place.

Sue had recommended Sarasota to us as a place where we would find lots of cultural activity and like-minded people to make friends with. She was so right. Both of us have been enjoying our friends, theater, symphony, golf and life at the club.

But all play didn't work for me, even in retirement. So in between theatre and golf and dinner dates, I have been teaching in the schools and writing. This is where you find me now, putting the finishing touches on my latest book.

She's on Fire

When we lived in Irish Catholic Jamaica Plain, my mother encouraged me to join my friends when they went

to church. It can't hurt you, she said. So I grew up knowing I was Jewish, even though I spent a lot of time at St.
Mary's. I didn't kneel or use Holy Water after my father
yelled at me for doing that, but I was very comfortable
among Catholics.

So I loved having Sister Kay Kay in my writing class in
the summers in Maine. The baseball cap on top of her habit
should have been the giveaway, had I realized there was
more to Sister than she gives away. But I never saw it as a
statement, just an eyeshade to protect her from the sun.

What you see in Sister is a serene, devoted, charming
nun. You see a woman of grace and talent, a woman who
writes music and performs it on one of her guitars or her
auto harp. She writes lyrics as well, relating her creations
to her devotion to God.

Sister thinks of others before she thinks of herself. She
is modest and peaceful, trained in obedience, a woman
who finds it easy to love, to listen, to care, and to help others ease their pain. She waters seeds to make them grow.

Imagine my surprise, then, even my shock, at seeing
sister, baseball cap and all, on the front page of the local
newspaper with the headline, "Nun Thwarts Burglary Bid
at Convent." Responding to a noise at 3:30 a.m. Sunday,
sister saw someone's fingers attempting to open a screen.
She slammed the window down on the fingers and hit the
panic button. The intruder escaped.

Picture our quiet, peace-loving nun, awakened from
sleep, seeing the fingers trying to pry open the screen, and
watch her become a lioness, protecting the other nuns,
asleep and unaware of danger. She slams the window,
alerts the police with her button, and no doubt begins to
think of the lyrics and melody that would fit this situation.

Too bad she didn't have a baseball bat to go with
the hat.

Passion and Risk

Like my mother, when I get really involved in something I believe in, I never worry about the possible consequences. When I was teaching fifth grade in the seventies the administration was looking for teachers of sex education, a highly volatile subject even then. Why not? I knew it was politically risky. There would be parents and others opposed and I could get some flak. But I knew how important it was for students who begin to think about sex, often without adult input. So I took the chance.

There were objections, like the mother who stormed into my classroom screaming, "Where's the S-E-X teacher?" I wasn't sure she spelled it so the students wouldn't understand or that she couldn't bring herself to say the word. The deal we made was that her daughter would go to the library during sex education class. I hope she found some good materials there.

Then, in retirement, I had another chance at relating to and educating young women in sex education. This time they were teen mothers of high school age. The risk was still there, for even parents of teens who had already had sex and/or babies were leery of their children being educated about contraception.

So, you might say, rest on your laurels. But, by retirement age, I realized that risk only heightened my passion instead of smothering it. If there were risk, then it most certainly was worth doing. So I interviewed teens, traveled to Europe, studied the research and wrote books about teen sexuality and the lack of education we provided.

Living in a retirement community led to my research on sexually transmitted diseases among the elderly. To my surprise I discovered that the over-fifty age group, up to and including people in their seventies and eighties, were at risk for STDs, including HIV and AIDS. They were a population whose statistics were equal to those of twenty- to thirty-year-olds.

I began by speaking with groups of elderly women, talking about risk-taking and protection, particularly among the recently single forming new relationships.

Even though they weren't comfortable asking a pro- spective partner if he or she had been tested for HIV/AIDS, speaking with that population was a comfortable place to be. No one objected to our discussions. I think perhaps because women didn't really believe the message.

Then came the real risk. I was invited to talk with a group of elderly men, at least half of whom were retired doctors. I struggled with that one. They could chew me up and spit me out. Who was this laywoman to tell them about STDs? I figured out my reply – I would deal with relation- ships, not medicine, and I would respect their knowledge.

I did it, arriving with booklets of information, male and female condoms, some colored and some flavored, stats, charts and graphs and a speech. They were wonder- ful! They left bearing my gifts and thanking me for letting them know about this important trend. It turned out to be fun, my passion undiminished. I hope I'll continue to enjoy facing risk, no matter how old I am.

A Wake-up Call, Sarasota FL, 2008

Excerpts from a Presentation
to Senior Males on HIV/AIDS

Thank you, gentlemen, for the opportunity to talk with you this morning about AIDS and the elderly. I have taught sex education to elementary, high school and college students and senior females. This is my first presentation to senior males, and it feels like trying to get into a fraternity. First let me tell you what this talk will be about and what it won't be about.

It will be about behavioral issues surrounding new relationships as we age. It will be about why seniors are at risk for HIV/AIDS, and why it's hard to talk about this risk with new partners. It's about protecting our partners and ourselves and it's about protecting your grandchildren by talking with them about unprotected sex. What it will not be about is the medical aspects of AIDS. It would be presumptuous of me to talk medical issues since I am not trained in that area and, as I look around at this group, I realize that many of you are. So, no medicine. Only behavior.

Most people are surprised to hear that HIV/AIDS is of concern to our age group. I was myself until I looked at the research and discovered that the over-fifty population is one of the fastest growing categories of people with AIDS. In the nineties, cases in our demographic rose twice as fast as among younger adults. And . . . the senior rate in Florida is the highest in the nation.

Safe sex is a foreign concept to seniors who have been with one partner for so long, far before the age of AIDS, seniors who stopped using condoms when there was no longer any possibility of getting pregnant. Yet, so many seniors are newly single, lonely, starting relationships with new partners, facing the same issues adolescents face when they start dating.

I haven't seen figures on this, but among our circle of friends are ten newly formed relationships. Perhaps it's the same for you.

We trust a new partner who may be an old friend. We would never question whether she had been monogamous. We would be   reluctant to ask if she had been tested for HIV.

But, assuming a new partner may have been monogamous during a marriage (not always true), with whom has your new partner been sexually involved during the interim before you began dating? And where has her partner been? To complicate these issues, Viagra has created a group of newly active elderly men.

Some of the reasons senior sex is not talked about are: ageism ignores the fact that seniors are sexual beings; doctors ignore symptoms of STDs since they don't believe that older seniors have sex; seniors attribute symptoms to aging, not illness; few studies are done on seniors; doctors and seniors are embarrassed to discuss sex together; seniors may be embarrassed to buy condoms.

In the United States we are condom-phobic, even though condom use, with the exception of abstinence, is the only proven method of decreasing the transmission of HIV/AIDS and other STDs. Unlike European countries which advertise them on billboards and have them available on every street corner and every public bathroom, the U.S. treats condoms as something to be avoided.

Use the wisdom of aging. Ask your partner questions, get tested and use condoms. Stay healthy and live to a riper old age.

And why do I think grandparents are a good resource for talking about unprotected sex with their grandchildren? I have recently published two books about teen pregnancy and sex education. During my research I learned that the two major deterrents for "at risk" adolescents are caring mentors (that's you) and education (that's you, too). So if you have the opportunity, take it.

Note to the reader: I ask myself why I so enjoy teaching and talking with groups of people and then I recall my mother's salons as she sewed, surrounded by people, listening to their problems and helping them find solutions. I so admired her ability to do this and I take pleasure in trying to do the same.

I'll Take Something Off
If You'll Put Something On –
Excerpts from My European Study Tour, 1998

The Netherlands opened my eyes. The Dutch are prag-
matists, surrounded as they are by their friend and enemy,
the sea. They have very liberal attitudes about religion,
education, sex and marijuana. Parents and schools accept
adolescent sexuality with the major caveat being no unprotected sex. There is almost universal knowledge of the dan-
gers of HIV/AIDS and other STDs and almost universal
access to contraception and information.

The Netherlands went through a dramatic change after
World War II. Prior to the war this was a country of large
families with strong religious values; sex was a big secret
and family planning was a sin. But the post-war generation
had the pill and information from TV and travel. It refused
to accept the traditional values and initiated a National Organization for Sexual Reform. Even the Catholic Church,
greatly outnumbered by opponents of religious control,
agreed that people should decide for themselves about the
size of their families.

There was also universal agreement that abortion
should be prevented if at all possible. Even though the
state paid for abortions, people really didn't want them.
Let's avoid the possibility, they said, through universal sex
education in the schools and universal access to family
planning and contraception. The church and the state didn't
interfere with the people and the people took responsibility
for themselves.

We learned all of this as we visited schools and clinics,
the red light district, the sex museum and family planning
centers. With the lowest rates of teen pregnancy in
developed countries, we were not surprised to learn that
close to ninety percent of teens used contraception at first

intercourse. It's the cultural expectation, supported by all
the adults in their lives. The media collaborate, producing
advertising campaigns with themes like the title of
this piece.

Their attitude was so refreshing when compared with
our unwillingness to discuss teen sexuality and our further
unwillingness to educate young people or support them in
developing safe sex habits. We saw many beautiful sites
and had many moving experiences, but the most exciting
of all was my introduction to Dutch morality. The only sin
was unprotected sex. When I returned from the study tour,
I wrote my second book on teen sex: *Safer Sex: the New
Morality* (Morning Glory Press, Buena Park CA, 2000).

The Day I Flunked Fingerprinting

No good deed goes unpunished. And so it was with my
volunteering to work for the Sarasota Public School System. If it were considered pure volunteering, there would
be no story, but because I receive an honorarium, I am an
employee, and that's where the fingerprinting comes in.

According to the Sarasota Police Department, in con-
junction with the School Department, all paid employees
must be fingerprinted at the office of the School Police in
the School Department Complex in the building with the
blue awning. This service is provided, but it is not free.
The employee must bring a money order or a cashier's
check in the amount of $96.00, money that will perhaps
be reimbursed by the department in which he/she works. I
did as I was bid, got the check, made the appointment, and
wended my way to the office of fingerprints.

"Yo," I said to the fine looking gentleman who turned
out to be an FBI retiree, "can you help me? Where is the
black ink pad?' I knew my way around fingerprinting because I had dipped into that black ink several years earlier

when working with incarcerated teen mothers.

His kind eyes crinkled as he said, "Old technology, Madame. Kindly put your fingers onto this TV screen."

Aha, I thought, clean and simple. There on the screen appeared my prints, or what appeared to be my prints. The gentleman sighed. He sighed again.

"Let's try it this way, dear Madame." He rolled each finger on the screen, producing much darker, much larger smudges, and I looked lovingly at my fingerprints. "Oh," he sighed. "No ridges."

"Where have all my ridges gone?" I asked him. "Why no ridges?"

He smiled again and picked up my application to check the birth date. "You have used up your ridges with work and play," he said. "Eighty years of use, and the ridges are gone. The FBI will want to reject you, but I will come to your aid. I will tell them I see a lovely lady, a teacher, a person of gentle years to be trusted with children. I will tell them to pass you even though you failed fingerprinting."

I gave him my check with my ridgeless fingers and it did not fail.

Allie – First among mentors.

Mentors

According to the research, the two most important factors that can influence an "at risk" child are education and a good mentor. I discovered this while writing books on teen pregnancy prevention, and I have since watched excellent mentors change young people's lives. But I have also discovered that mentoring is beneficial not only for young people; it is also lifesaving for older people, "at risk" people who are working out problems or are thrust into new jobs and are floundering. In this section I'd like to honor some of the mentors who made a big difference in my life. I don't mention my mother, my first mentor, since she appears throughout the book.

To: Tom
From: Evelyn Lerman
Re: Greetings and references
On: 1/17/07

Dear Tom:

I think of you so often, when reading a great book, when seeing a gorgeous sunset, a rainbow, when celebrating life-changing events, when "doing my homework" by touching all bases before a meeting, even when just driving to school to teach. And it's always with joy and appreciation for you being in my life, for giving me the opportunity to be your Vice Principal and to learn from your leadership.

We have just had the unspeakably emotional experience of seeing Susan married to a wonderful Brit, Ian. The wedding was Sunday at sunset on the Bay in Sarasota on the grounds of an old estate. The wedding was officiated by Carol Altarescu, my first student teacher at Runkle, who filled in for her husband who came down with pneumonia two days before the wedding. Carol was superb, even quieting the crowd of a hundred with just a flick of her little finger when they began clapping before the end. The finale was – sit down for this one – the "I now pronounce you, by the power vested in me by the . . . ," no other booming voice than that of dear Albert who became a notary public for the occasion. Not a dry eye in the place, and much laughter combined with the tears. Becca was here from Afghanistan and spoke, along with Ian's children, some by webcam. It was a twenty-first century wedding in a twentieth century estate, mixing Church of England with Judaism amidst orchids and palm trees. Well, this wasn't the purpose of the email, but once I had you I couldn't resist sharing.

I have just applied for a teaching position at Manatee Community College where they have begun a new program, that of training teachers who are coming out of industry in mid-life, just as Albert did. I thought it such a wonderful program and I think I have the skills and experience to do the training that I decided to apply, even though my references, and I, are far too old. I put you down as one of my supervisors and as a reference. You may never hear from Dr. Susan Sheffield, but in the event you do I just thought I'd prepare you.

Hope this finds you, Pam, your beautiful family, and the Baker family, all in good spirits, good health, and enjoying life. We surely are. On February 10 we leave for Antarctica, a dream Allie has had for a long time. Of course I am cold in air conditioning, but he is outfitting me for the Antarctic and having so much fun doing it that I'm getting into the spirit.

Love and thanks,

Ev

Louise

I was Director of English for the Brookline Public Schools. Not quite my mother's goal for me – she wanted me to be president of the United States – but not bad for a woman who came to education at the age of forty. Under the supervision of Louise, my role model and my mentor, I began to learn what being an independent woman really meant. Louise was there as supporter, questioner, clarifier, and I was there as a novice administrator learning the ropes. There really were ropes, ropes on which you could climb to the sky, or ropes on which you could hang yourself.

When Louise and I met biweekly she asked me to keep a running list of projects on which I was working. Document the projects, she said, with comments and any relevant papers. I stuffed these into a manila file folder; they became the agenda for our meetings. The lists ran up to twenty-five topics, and some weeks our meetings lasted about an hour. Two minutes per complicated project made

for frenetic meetings, but we both loved them. We whipped
through the politics, the economics, the philosophies and
the psychologies of each in split second fashion, often talking shorthand. There were no barriers to our communica-
tion, no secrets. Nothing embarrassed us and we seemed to
be reading each other's minds as we talked. Nothing had
ever felt more like talking with my mother than did these
meetings with Louise.

Then she got to feelings. How was it going? What was
I feeling? I learned "I messages" and the most important
thing about guilt that I'll ever know. The guilt comes first.
After one potentially ugly meeting with K-2 teachers, I
was feeling defeated. I got them angry, I said. You can't,
she said. I marveled. Of course I can. All my life I have
been able to get people angry, happy, satisfied, whatever.
No, she said. People have a share in what happens to them.
If you are a friend of someone you will avoid behaving
in ways that you know from experience annoy him or
her. However, whether they get angry or not after some
behavior of yours is up to them. They have a choice. You
will choose to behave as you wish and they will choose
to behave as they wish. In other words, I didn't have the
total responsibility any more for every interaction. What
a burden was lifted from me! How many years had I been
carrying that weight around, worrying that every move I
made caused sorrow or joy or frustration. Now, though I
still had a share of the outcome, I didn't have it all. I was
not God, she told me. I loved it.

The "I" message works like this. If you are upset by
something someone has said or done, you go to the person
and you tell them: When you do (describe the action), I
feel (describe your feeling) because it (your own reaction).
An example comes easily. When the supervisor I trusted
least wrote a memo to Louise and sent cc's to all the

honchos in the system, including me, I was upset. It touched on testing policy and should have come from the Department rather than from her. I felt embarrassed because it made me look as if I had no idea what was going on in my department and I felt like a fool. I gathered courage to talk with her even though I was unsure of her motivation. Did she intend to shaft me or did she see it as her prerogative to go to the top when she worked rather than to work through and with the Department? I never really found out, but I did give her an "I message." It helped, I think, as we managed to build up a grudging respect for each other. I still didn't trust her, but at least I knew we could work together.

Louise's insights were so important to me as an educator, an administrator and a human being negotiating life with my loved ones that I still use the lessons I learned all those years ago.

Louis Harris

When I was a young married woman with children in Hebrew school, they came home and asked me to help them. Alas, I couldn't read Hebrew because I hadn't been trained. So I went to our temple classes for adults and there I had the good fortune to find Mr. Harris. He was a gifted and talented Hebrew teacher to whom I reported every Monday morning. This saintly and scholarly teacher of Hebrew was also a student of Greek and Latin. His Hebrew lived through him and for him. "To write," he said. The Hebrew letters are . . . but, if we add one letter and harden the word, it now becomes "to inscribe" as on cement or marble. Just one letter, how marvelous! I fell in love with Mr. Harris, with the Hebrew, and with the idea of going back to school as an adult. Mr. Harris started me on my careers.

I digress here to tell you about my first day in this hallowed class. I introduced myself "Gveret Lerman (Mrs. Lerman) and this dear little man put his hands to his grey head and rocked.

His sparkly blue eyes clouded over, peering through the thick lenses of his glasses. "From Albert?" he asked. I said yes and he groaned. "Oh. God forbid. Another such student? Please God, no. He should live and be well."

I asked him to tell me why he was so upset, although I knew in my soul that Allie must have been a terrible student in Hebrew School because he was not the sort to take after-school sessions well. Mr. Harris scarcely knew him because he and the other boys would dutifully check into his class and then, when he opened the book, out they ran to the playground where the baseball game was in progress.

"In and out," Mr. Harris intoned. "Oy, vey."

I assured him that I would be good, that I would come to class and learn, that I would do my homework, that I loved learning; thus began my love affair with adult learning that grows stronger and more fulfilling each year.

Louis Harris, elderly scholar, one time teacher of reluctant children, was now enriching the lives of adults during his declining years. But he was only declining physically. Mentally and intellectually he was more brilliant than many I have since studied with. He made the verb to write live for me. He explained its literal meaning, its extended meanings, its meaning in Hebrew in its simple form and its meaning in its stronger form. Inscribe was in stone; paper was only temporary.

I think I really believe though, in my deepest heart, that even on paper writing is forever. Once it's down, it's inscribed. As a teacher now, I tell my writers that to write is not to inscribe, that the first draft is loose, is reusable, is throwoutable, is retractable. But I don't think I really believe it, and I wonder if they do, either.

But Mr. Harris's other lessons – the history of Hebrew and of the Hebrews, the sociology and the archeology of Israel and of the Jews, the philosophy and the psychology, the art and the music, the relationship and interrelationships of the Jews and their God, of the Hebrew, Greek, and Latin. Though he loved his Greek and Latin, he did not cherish them the way he did the Hebrew. He was first and foremost a Jew, then a teacher. I am told he spent his last years at the Hebrew Home for the Aged where he held classes daily for the residents. He was a scholar to the end, sharing his beautiful mind with others.

Carol

My first student teacher smiled at me. Here I was, a few days before school opened, heroically trying to get the portable classroom ready for the kids, a task which felt insurmountable. I smiled back as best I could, straining to move the three-drawer metal file that I couldn't budge.

"Where do you want it?" Carol asked.

"Over in that corner," I panted. "Let's call for some help."

Carol put her shoulder to the file, giving it a tremendous shove. The file knew it had met its master and obligingly sailed over into the corner.

I gasped. She was half my size and had moved a mountain. "What else do you know how to do?" I asked her.

"Just about anything I have to," said Carol, and our lifelong friendship began.

The fourth graders arrived, most of them pliable and pleasant, but there was one very tall, angry boy who didn't fit in. He needed to be noticed, so he began throwing his weight around by yelling at the smaller children and reluctantly doing what I told him.

Carol took him on. Though he was twice her size, she cornered him, looked up into his face, and threatened him with terrible consequences if he didn't shape up. He did. Like the file, he had met his master. Carol and I learned how to be teachers that year, but I know she taught me more than I taught her.

Her mentoring might have ended there, but we became such good friends that we have continued to learn from each other ever since. Carol is an artist with an exquisite sense of taste, so she taught me how to recognize beautiful things. She is talented with all things electronic, and frequently gets me out of trouble on my computer.

But most of all, Carol's endless love for both Allie and me embraced her husband Howard and her three children. So we have an extended family that continues to teach us about love.

Albert

F . . . it! That's Albert speaking and here is how he fits into this picture. For sixty-five years he has been teaching me to f . . . it, or them, as the case may be. He is the world's best survivor. Don't lay it on me, he says, and refuses to let anyone do it to him. I, who have always been overly willing to bear the burden for all interactions, am married to a man who will not touch even a corner of the pack of woe for which he feels no responsibility. It's not that he's irresponsible. On the country, he's one of the most responsible people I know. But he chooses his responsibilities carefully and he does not choose them, too. No one can give them to him. He's a wonderful combination of sensitivity and insensitivity, generosity of spirit and selectivity of words, warmth and frigidity, intellectual brilliance in his ability to clutch the heart of an issue and practicality in his rejection of all things which smack of phoniness.

But the most wondrous part of his personality is his integrity. He is honest about everything including himself and never at odds about this. It gets him into trouble as you might guess because he tells the truth always. There is no room for concern about the recipient's feelings. He really believes it's up to him or her to deal with the truth and it's up to Al to tell it. This is not always politic or diplomatic, but it surely is clear. You know where you stand all the time.

This integrity has another effect on the people in Al's sphere. You'd better be clear about your own goals. Don't confuse your motivation or muddy your objectives. State your problem clearly and precisely and don't confuse the issue.

Now there is a problem here. Not everyone is blessed with the ability to do this well and he's not always patient with those folks, including me. On the other hand, he does get people to do it and this is where he's done the most for me. When I get muddy, Al clears the waters. He's a clarifier in my life.

He is also my lover as I am his. What makes one and one more than two? Brought up to cherish relationships, I was fortunate enough to marry a man who also cherished the marriage vow. I've wondered about this question many times, most often when I observe good, fair and poor marriages. Where is the point at which two entities merge to become a third entity, each entity still unique and important? It's the moments during which the two together become more than the two apart; the partnership has magic in it.

Albert taught me so much of this. I have been blessed, not only with a wonderful husband, but also with a powerful mentor.

Ev and Al at Becca and Toby's wedding.

Travel

Allie and I had always loved to travel, but when we were working as camp directors and teachers we had precious little time to spare. Our trips were short but sweet, always during school vacations.

When we retired, first from camp and then from school, we had the time, the desire, the money, and the good health to really go for it.

"I have had enough of museums, art galleries and churches," said my darling as we looked over catalogues for travel. "I want some adventure."

Most of the time he was packed and ready while I dithered a little. Would I be warm enough? Would I be able to do the activities and not hold him up?

He reassured me, locked the luggage, and then off we went.

Armed with his spirit, I even mustered the courage to travel without him.

Study Tour to Europe
July 25, 1998
2 p.m. at Logan Airport

She would have been 100 years old today if she had lived. What would Ceil say about my trip? What would she have thought about my two-week Study Tour to Europe, to the Netherlands, Germany and France to find out why the European countries are so much better at preventing teen pregnancy than is the United States? Would she have approved of my leaving my husband of fifty-one years, the first time either of us has done this except when Al traveled on business those many years ago?

It's hard to guess what her reaction would have been, since three of her very strong values are competing here: her "one man, one family, one God" loyalty; her devotion to education; her devotion to the welfare of children. In this case I think the education and children values would have won out.

My body and my mind put up a terrible struggle before this day came, this day which finds me on my way to Philadelphia to meet the Tour Group, and then to fly to Amsterdam. When Jeanne, my publisher (as distinguished from Jeanne, my mother-in-law) called and asked me if I'd like to go, I talked it over with Allie and we both agreed it was a good idea for me to continue my research into teen pregnancy prevention. My first book on the subject had just been published, and I was hot.

So it was a done deal, I thought. All that was left was to buy the ticket, send the tour director the money for the trip and the accommodations while there, and wait for the itinerary. No problems there. But the body, divorcing itself completely from the workings and plannings of the mind, took its own route as the anxiety of the reality set in.

There would be no competent husband to hold the tickets, no Allie to lead the way through the airports, no strong arms to load the luggage onto airplanes and buses, no one to lift luggage over sidewalks or put the suitcase on the bed, no Al to tip, grip and schlepp. All of this had to be done, and I was the one who was going to do it. Doesn't sound terrible, I know, but with tendonitis and arthritis in both wrists, arthritic fingers on the right hand, a tricky lower back, a chronic stiff neck, a diverticulosis-ridden gut, an asthmatic chest – my fear was that any one of those stress points could flip under the weight of the decision making and baggage lugging.

Not liking to think about the issues, and not willing to admit to most of them, I had made the plans fully convinced I would be fine and could manage without my compassionate lover/helper. And so I continued to think until the week before takeoff when I came down with a sore throat and cough.

That would have been enough to terrify me, but the body continued to take over. Next came the upset stomach, then the heartburn, then the diarrhea. And, finally, the sciatic nerve down the left side of the leg. Each area was competing with the others for the pain and suffering prize, and I think they were in a perfect tie.

Yet here I am, having conquered most of my demons, fought my way through the body unbeautiful, sitting on a 17-passenger Business Express, drinking bottled water and eating pretzels. In a few hours I meet the group, my Jeanne the Publisher, Barbara the tour director and advocate for children, plus twenty other adult advocates from all parts of the pregnancy prevention world, and twenty students from the University of North Carolina. Our age range will be from twenty to eighty, mostly female, all looking for solutions to the teen pregnancy problems in our country.

Ceil would have been pleased and proud.

A Blank Page

I find a blank page in the journal I wrote while on the teen sex study tour, and I read on. Finally there is a note:

I need to write up Cologne, Germany, but it was such a painful experience that I have been avoiding it.

Having been a teenager when World War II was ending and having read about and seen the pictures of the concentration camps during the movie news, I was so anxious about going to Germany that I think I would have made a scene even if one hadn't happened on its own.

Let me try to recreate Cologne for you. It is a beautiful city with a magnificent cathedral that we visited in the morning. Tired and hungry, we found a lovely beer garden restaurant with outdoor seating in an area surrounded by flowers. The headwaiter sat about twelve of us at a table and the waiter arrived soon to take our orders. It was a complicated order with so many of us, but he seemed to have it right in spite of our limited German and his limited English.

When he came with the orders he barked out the plates, not remembering who ordered what. One of my tour mates and I had ordered the same salad and we both spoke up. He began yelling in German. My limited Yiddish helped me translate his diatribe into "idiot women, stupid Americans, etc.," but all I really heard was "Dirty Jew." I began to cry, excused myself from the table, and ran to the bus.

My wonderful publisher/friend Jeanne left the table to

console me. She put her arm around me and I cried onto her shoulder for what seemed like a long time. I cried for all the Jews in the concentration camps; I cried for all the Jews who died, especially for the children; I cried for myself for the privilege of being a first generation American. When I had cried myself out, I thanked Jeanne and composed myself for the ride back to Paris.

Ellis Island II, 2003

The plane was landing at LaGuardia Airport, right on time. I took out my cell phone and dialed Rebecca's cell phone. "I'm here, darling," I whispered, for I'd lost my voice twenty-four hours before, the beginning of an upper respiratory infection. "Just exiting the plane and on my way to luggage. Should be there in about an hour."

Becca laughed. "It's OK, Grandma," she said. "I'll hike to Ground Zero and do some exploring. I'll be waiting for you at Castle Clinton in Battery Park. Stay in touch."

I was really here, on my way to Ellis Island, eighty-three years after my mother, father, and sister landed here. It had been a dream of mine for years, this trip to Ellis Island. My two sisters and I had put up plaques for Mother, Daddy and Miriam, and I wanted to see them.

No voice, I thought. She had no language. She had a baby in her arms, and a sick husband by her side. She had one cardboard suitcase and the clothes on her back. She had one large feather quilt, her only possession from the Old Country, and she had hopes. Castles in the Air, she called her dreams.

And here I was about to meet my granddaughter, Rebecca, her middle name my mother's, and her heart and soul my mother's as well. I laughed to myself as I thought about how we all got here. Mother came steerage on the last boat that brought Russian immigrants to this country before the Russian scare shut down our borders. Becca was coming on the Chinatown Bus from Boston.

"Ten dollars each way, Grandma. You can get on if all the Chinese have places. It goes every hour on the hour from Chinatown Boston to Chinatown New York. And it's a beautiful bus and they show movies for three and a half hours."

I was on the Portland, Maine-LaGuardia leg of my $500 ticket from Florida to Maine to New York to Florida and Becca was already there with her little backpack while I was schlepping my bags en route to the taxi stand to get to our friend's house to leave the luggage. Ceil's brothers had sent her the $50.00 for her passage from England to Boston. Becca surely had the best deal of all. Leave it to the young ones to figure it out.

The taxi line snaked around the block when I finally reached it and my heart sank. I'll never get there before it closes, I thought. Ceil must have felt the same thing.

--I'll never get through Ellis Island to the land that I see through these windows, mumbled Ceil to herself. Something will stop us. The baby will cough or they will see something wrong with my husband's eyes. They will notice his limp. She didn't talk out loud because she didn't want Meyer to know she was worried.

I won't make it before it closes, I thought to myself, just as an attractive young man in a blue shirt smiled at me.

"Can I help you, Madam? Where would you like to go?"

I could speak the language but I had no idea where Seventy-Eighth Street was or how far away. I knew I was hot and tired and the luggage was heavy. I decided he looked clean and honest, how do you ever know, and I asked him how much it would cost to go to the address I had before me.

'Only forty-five dollars, madam, plus tolls and tip, " he said. "Don't worry. I'll take care of you."

I wondered if that meant cement shoes in the ocean while he made off with my luggage and pocketbook, but it was this gypsy cabbie or not getting there at all. Hey, if my mother could take her chances across the Atlantic I could take mine across Manhattan. He got me there, and after my stories about my immigrant parents – he too was an immigrant, he from the Dominican Republic – he said he wouldn't charge me for tolls. He took my luggage to the doorman, and headed for the Battery – only fifteen dollars more, Madame, and my heart lifted. Becca was calling to reassure me we'd make it and she'd be waiting and I cheerfully paid him his sixty dollars plus a generous tip for all his helpfulness. When I told the story to New York friends they laughed with tears in their eyes.

"Ev," they told me, "the fare is normally twenty dollars to our house, although fifteen to the Battery was just right."

In retrospect, I would have given him a hundred just to get there on time. And my mother and father both worked months for my uncles just to pay them back the fifty dollars they had advanced for their trip.

Finally at Battery Park, Becca found at Castle Clinton, we got into line for the ferry. The sun was beating down on us as we waited for an hour to board. My hat, so carefully packed in Maine, was in the luggage at Maida's house. The paper I had brought to do the rubbing of the plaques was also in the luggage, so I wasn't prepared on both counts, but I had my granddaughter, a bit of shade and hope. The ferry made up for all the discomfort, a beautiful boat on a beautiful day with a beautiful view of the Statue of Liberty, heart-stopping even after all the pictures we've seen.

When she looked at the Statue she may have said, --Here is my home. Here we will be safe. Here my children will be educated.

Ellis Island, especially the crowded Great Room, was everything I'd wished for. The hopes and dreams of the European immigrants who filled these rooms overpowered us as we looked at pictures, saw the original desk at which immigrants were registered, and envisioned what they felt when they looked through the windows at the New York skyline. The Golden Land was theirs, if only they could cross the water to the land. We found the plaques, the Gift Shop was selling packets of paper and pencils to do rubbings, and we spent a glorious hour absorbing Ellis Island. Becca and I held hands on the trip back to the Battery. We had done it and we had done it together. It was our dream come true.

Old Cheese and New Wine

Old cheese and new wine combined with old songs in a new place as our guide escorted my husband and me to the party. It was early in the 1950's when Allie and I were in the hills of Austria, at a Heuriger, a celebration of the first pouring of the new wine.

The people, dressed in traditional clothes that they wore with pride, carried heavy casks of wine, thick loaves of country bread and huge wheels of aged cheese. Some carried accordions and it was around them that all gathered, singing old country songs, clapping and swaying with the music.

I knew just enough German to recognize some of the words, but much too much Yiddish to be comfortable singing. The Austrians would surely pick up my accent and we would be exposed as Jews. It was too soon after World War II for us to be comfortable with that. Austria: the home of such beauty, such happiness and so much painful history.

I kept silent.

Chateau Lake Louise

The image framed by my window
At Chateau Lake Louise
Captures my eyes, my heart and my soul.
The craggy mountains on the left
The soaring pines on the right
The green, glacial water in the center
The majestic glacier pouring its runoff into the Lake
One look is not enough.

As the sun rises higher
As the clouds cover the sun
As the light flickers on and off
I look again.
The beauty is indescribable
Time becomes timeless
Life is on hold.

Why Antarctica?
Antarctica Journal
Copyright by Evelyn Lerman, March 2, 2007

"Where are you going on your trip?"

"Antarctica," I say, and the eye rolling begins. "WHY

did you choose Antarctica?"

"I didn't. I chose Allie, and he chose Antarctica."

But they surely knew that before they asked, because I am cold in air-conditioned Florida. No one ever sees me indoors without an added layer, a sweater, a jacket, or a shawl. So when they asked why I chose Antarctica, I'm certain they thought they knew the answer already.

I could see it in their eyes. Or their false smiles. Or their eye rolls.

> *He is making her go.*
> > *She won't let him out of her sight.*
> > > *She can't say no to him.*
> > > > *She likes being a martyr.*

Although they were sure they knew the answer, they hadn't got it right. The truth is I married an adventurer and he married a woman who was up to any intellectual challenge, but had no appetite for any physical challenge, even the tiniest one. My daily trip to the health club for thirty minutes of aerobics and stretching in the pool is the outer limit of my physical output. And that's only because my will to keep physically fit is stronger than my reluctance to exercise.

Yet here was my husband, talking up Antarctica with a twinkle in his eye and a bounce in his step. Catalogs filled with outdoor gear were pouring in. Websites for travel were visited. The travel agent was consulted. People who had been there were sought out and talked with. No source of information was ignored. And the twinkle and the bounce grew more pronounced.

On all our previous adventure trips we had spoken with fellow travelers, as fellow travelers do – once the hellos and where are you froms have been concluded – asking what trips they had taken. And then, always, the question, "What one stood out from all the others? What trip would you recommend?" Invariably, whether old or young, elegant or plain, of whatever nationality or race, male or female, the answer was "Antarctica."

And we would ask, "Why?"

Their answers were remarkably similar. In fact, there was no answer. They just couldn't say. "Well," they'd begin, "it was awe-inspiring. Or, it was special. Or different. Or wonderful." But no one was able to put into words what made it any of those things. Even so, Allie wondered, could so many experienced travelers be wrong?

When I began to think about my reasons to go to Antarctica. I came up with four. First, every trip Allie has ever suggested, and to which I have reluctantly agreed, has been extraordinary. I climbed Machu Picchu ("Rocky" in Peru!), I marveled in Africa, I got into and out of zodiacs in the Galapagos to see the giant turtles, I was delighted with the ever-changing vistas in the Canadian Rockies, and always I was happy that I went. So one answer would be that I trusted him to select something special. Second, perhaps even more motivational, is that when Al is engaged to his fullest, in whatever venture he has chosen, it thrills me to share his delight. He lives life so richly that it rubs off on me. Third and fourth, there were the challenges: physical, to find out if I could really do this cold and demanding thing; intellectual, to see if I could put the "why" into words.

My first reason for agreeing to go to Antarctica was right. This trip was more than special. He had chosen something spectacular.

As I write this now, in our fortieth hour on board the

Explorer II, we have arrived at the tip of the Antarctic Peninsula. The quantity and quality of the ice surrounding the ship is such that the Captain cannot allow us to land in the zodiacs. So we go out in the zodiacs to explore the icebergs and the sea ice, to see our first fur seal, to observe the many species of birds, and to experience the Antarctic cold, dressed in four layers, topped off with a huge red parka and life jacket. And we are not cold. The real adventure will begin when we can pull into Paulet Island, and the zodiacs can take us to shore, where we will wade into the water in our magnificent knee high boots reminiscent of the galoshes of our youth, to pick our way along the rocky shores of Antarctica. My gear, courtesy of my magnificent provisioner-husband, keeps me warm and dry.

The second reason was right, too. Not only did his enthusiasm rub off on me, I developed my own.

And the challenges? Physically, I did it all, marveling at how well I felt in this dry, pristine environment with no allergies, little arthritis, good food and lots of rest. Intellectually? Could I put it into words? You, the reader, will decide.

Why? It's the Light

At this time of year the sun comes up at 5:00 a.m. and sets at 9:00 p.m., affording sixteen hours of daylight. The wonder of this light is not just the duration; it's the variation. It changes everything, minute by minute, whether the ship is underway or at anchor, whether we are on board, in the zodiac, or on the shore of an island or on the continent itself.

A rock-topped glacier reaches for the gray of the sky, surrounded by layers of dappled clouds striped gray and

The Antarctica light changes everything minute by minute.

blue. A cap of thick gray suffuses the scene, short rays of
sun frosting the snow. But wait. As the Explorer II floats
by, the glacier begins to disappear from view and the light
changes again. The blue is gone, covered by the gray cap
pulling its flaps down over the ears of rock peeking out of
the top. The sun is creeping out between the layers of snow
cover, creating craters of light and shadow. Now the scene
shifts and the blue water turns dark purple, bordering the
shadowed whiteness of the ice. Rock reaches out to sea, ice
reaches up to sun, clouds reach down to peaks, light frosts
the ice highlighting the blue crevasses.

It's the Day and the Night

The daily rhythms here in Antarctica are changed by
the length of the day and the shortness of the night. The

sun rises, flooding the cabin with light, even if the day
is cloudy. Let there be but a sliver of space between the
drapes, and a shaft of light penetrates the cabin, signaling
wake up time. The expectation of an early sunset after an
early sunrise is not met, but the body adjusts. As the ship
serves some type of food every few hours, the body reverts
to infancy – eat, sleep, eat, sleep, rock, toddle a bit, then
back to nap time.

It's the Glaciers

Towering two to three thousand feet above the sea, clus-
tering in peak after peak, the magnificent glaciers test the
waters with their thick fingers of ice. Blue-tinged crevasses
line up to see which can longer withstand the force of the
ice behind it. Stubborn and willful, the huge chunks hold
onto the mother glacier, determined to cling to the end. But
the weight becomes overpowering, and with the mighty
roar of childbirth, the ice calves into the sea, burrowing
into the depths and churning the water into huge waves. As
it finds its balance and rights itself, the tip emerges, leaving
the rest of its massive weight to explore the depths where it
hibernates until it's time to change places with the tip, roll
over, and emerge to the light of day. Uncompromising yet
flexible, the glaciers dominate Antarctica, threatening yet
nurturing the earth.

It's the Icebergs

Standing in the stern of the zodiac and holding the
rudder of the powerful motor that pushes these ten-seater
rubber boats is a young, strong naturalist, a member of
the Expedition Crew. He or she pilots the craft through
the sea ice with expert knowledge of shifting ice, all the

while informing us about the natural world around us. This morning's scheduled one-mile trip to the island turned out to be three miles by zodiac because the sea ice required the ship to move. It was cold but sunny, and the passengers were huddled up and quiet. But the scenery and the narration woke everyone up as magnificent icebergs, giant-sized, large, and small, dotted the sea. Tabular bergs, flat as a table, vied with artistic ice sculptures created by wind and water.

Winter Carnival sculptures can't compare to these creatures of the glacier, the sea, the wind, and the sun. When the first artist, the glacier, reluctantly, and with a giant roar, lets its pup go, the sea takes over to caress the huge body of ice in its grip, while the wind works its magic on the tip. Tired of the image, the iceberg shifts its weight, rolls over on its side, and brings its hidden parts to the surface, burying its face in the depths of the water. The sun, not to be outdone, frosts the bergs with a glisten of sparkles. Modernism, humanism, anthropomorphism, animism – each piece vying for the first prize. The penguins and the seals, wondrous in their own right, seemed commonplace today as the glacier, the sea, the wind, and the sun partnered to dazzle us.

It's the Adelie Penguins

But the penguins were not to be outdone by the scenery. The Adelie penguin chicks, looking like extras in the "March of the Penguins," were holding court when we landed today.

The sun had settled on the snow, hot enough to form small pools of water of just the right depth for the penguins to frolic in. And frolic they did. These enchanting creatures played King of the Mountain, Follow the Leader, My Wings Flap Better Than Your Wings, Watch Me! as they took what might have been their first baths. Behind us as we watched, a line of newly fledged chicks stood waiting for their parents to come for them. They had left their nests, but were only this far away when they decided they weren't quite ready to go it on their own. So they stood and waited.

It's the Guano

I thought I had discovered the magic – what it is that has people glassy eyed with emotion when they recommend Antarctica. It's the guano. You can smell it from the Promenade Deck on the ship as it anchors off the Island. Penguins, being nature's creatures, ingest, digest, and egest. They eat krill, their plentiful, local crustacean, and egest guano, which covers the island from the sea to the glacier. Penguins dot the island, wallpapering the hill from its rocky shore to its rocky top. Too plentiful to count, they follow nature's command to be fruitful and multiply, to feed their young, and to cover their world with guano. After our hike over the rocky, guano-covered shore, our waterproof boots needed to be immersed in the sea water, brushed by the guano meter, and scrubbed by the patient crew on shore before we could return to the relative safety and comfort of our seats on the zodiac which transports us to our home, the ship.

It's the Seals

Could be, but I think all seals are not as universally loved as are the penguins.

Dark brown fur seals are cuddly, alone or playing in

twos and threes. They are social, stretching their bodies and raising their heads as they hear noises nearby. They ignore the penguins who are curious about them, and appear contented to lie on the ice, take an occasional dip in the frigid water, and sleep.

Wedell seals, large and gray, are solitary souls. They stretch, full blubbery, on the iceberg, six hundred pounds turning over to let the sun warm white underbellies, then over again to share the warmth with their backs. Sunning on their favorite tabular icebergs, they are alone but not lonely.

Leopard Seals, large, long and lanky, nearly black, never quite at rest as they seek their prey in the water. Lying on the ice, on the lookout for the newly fledged penguin out testing water skills, they spot an unwary chick. Grasping the chick in strong jaws, they thrash him about until he is skinned and ready to eat. Surfeit after eating six or seven of these little ones, the Leopard Seal, unlike most members of the animal kingdom save man, kills a few more for sport.

It's hard to love the Leopard Seal, but you have to respect him.

It's a New Respect for the Senses

The visitor to the unknown planet at the bottom of the world develops a new respect for the senses.

The landscape beggars description with its limited palette of black, white and gray. But no, there are browns and greens and yellows and blues. They greet the eye later, when there is time to adjust to the rock and the ice and the sea and the sky. There are the blues embedded in the ice; there the greens and yellows growing on the rocks. The towering glaciers loom wedding cake white with peaks of marshmallow fluff poking into the sky. The chocolate of the rock pushes through, here and there hinting at the cobalt blue stone amidst the lichen and moss. As the sun slides out from behind a cloud the purple water turns blue and the opaque ice, growlers, and bergs become crystals reflecting the full spectrum. A new respect for the endless aspects of light and color is born, a new respect for the sense of sight.

The rocky promontory brimming with penguins appears to house a colony, a flock. But a closer look reveals families as baby chicks call for their parents and mothers and fathers seek their children. The calls are soft or loud, monotone or multitone. When a match is heard, the babies are fed and a quiet peace settles over the area. The visitor develops a new respect for sound.

Guano is guano, you might think. It smells the way it is supposed to smell, just as human waste does. But no, there is guano and guano. Depending on the amount, the dryness or wetness of the soil and rock, the concentration or the spread, guano has its own smell factor from one to ten. The smell becomes a part of the environment. The visitor develops a new respect for smell.

It's a New Respect for Knowledge

Here, too, we develop a new respect for knowledge. To the Captain we entrust our safety. He knows the wind and the water. He knows the ice, where it is and how it is, and he allows his ship to go only where it and the passengers will be safe. We give him our trust because he knows.

To the tour director we look for direction. He keeps us informed and in line. He will not allow us to stray. He knows the program and he knows people. He will tell us just enough each step of the way to get us through. The passengers become one instrument in his orchestra. We do what he tells us because he knows.

To the expedition director and team we entrust ourselves to succeed. The director will make sure we are safe as we transfer to the zodiacs and as we land on the beaches. He will show us how to navigate the terrain with the least amount of difficulty, and he will make sure we are given all the information about the environment that we need in order to fully enjoy it.

To the instruction team – the historian, the geographer, the geologist, the naturalists, and all the other academics and researchers who instruct us on the ship – we entrust our minds. They keep us as mentally fit as their fellow specialists keep us physically fit so we can enjoy all the wonders of the environment.

And our fellow passengers, from mountain men to professors, from bankers to editors, from world travelers to newly fledged adventurers, we respect something in each. They have selected this trip over all others, seeking, as we are, another view of the natural world.

It's the Environment

Above all, we have developed a respect for the environment, not only for what there is, but also for what there is not. We respect the absence of people, noise, pollution, visual impediments to the natural world, motor vehicles, exhaust, buildings, macadam, blazing color, lights beyond natural light, shopping malls, highways. All there is to see is what nature put here, rock, snow, wind, water, light, sky, sun, moon, stars, animals, and ice. We also respect the absence of conflict except for the natural state of predator and prey. Here men do not inhabit the world, except for the few science stations, and they seek only knowledge. Here there are no fights over land, territory, oil, gas, minerals, coal, religion. A multination agreement has outlawed sealing and whaling. Wild life is free to roam, to mate, to parent their young. The lack of violence, the lack of green, the lack of politicking, the lack of competition, combine with the environment to suffuse the visitor with a feeling of calm, of peace, of purity. The natural world has stripped us of vanity, of pride, and of the thirst for control and power. In Antarctica, we and the world are at peace.

It's a Feeling

Why Antarctica?

It's all of the above, of course, but it's more. It's not just the wildlife, not just the dry cold, not just vertical waves and horizontal seas, not just scenery, not just the absence of civilization and not just the presence of the pristine world – Antarctica is a feeling unlike any other we have experienced in previous trips.

In the capitals of Europe we marveled at the Uffizi Gallery, the lustrous beauty of the Bernini sculptures, the timeless wonder of the Pieta, the towering glory of the cathedrals and the Papal Palace, the incandescence of the Michelangelo works. In the Galapagos we thrilled to the scale of the giant turtles, the closeness of the marine life as they brushed past the zodiacs, the clarity of the air and the sky. At Machu Picchu we exalted at the climb to the ruins and the history embedded in the rock, we reveled in the coca tea and the charm of the Inca population. In the Canadian Rockies we thrilled at each new vista as the bus maneuvered the steep climbs and harrowing descents in the mountain peaks and valleys. We sampled the glacial water as our brains imprinted the beauty of the glacier dropped into the sea between the backdrop of twin mountains. And in Africa we throbbed with the excitement of each animal sighting – the lion, the gazelle, the leopard, the elephant, the hyena, the dik-dik, and the huge threatening rhino.

But Antarctica – the feelings we had were unlike any other. Never had we been so awed by setting – by the scale of the ice, the glaciers, the icebergs, the growlers, and the chunks of sea ice in sizes large and small. Ice as big as city blocks, as small as a beach pebble. Never so awed by limited color, by white in every shade, by black in every depth, by gray in every iteration, and by blues from deep azure to powder blue and every color chip in between. Awed by the amount of ice, mountains of it surrounding us on all sides, and carpets of it surrounding the zodiacs and the ship. Awed by the contrasts from the sky to the sea, by the ever-changing light and its duration, changing color, clarity, and texture. Awed by the vigor of the cold and by the warmth of the sun. Elated by the naturalness of the world. Delighted with the energy of the forces of nature. Lulled by the calm and the quiet, the beauty and subtlety, by the absence of clamor and clash.

Why Antarctica? Because, having experienced Antarctica with all of our senses, we will never see the world the same way again.

What's Next?

Epilogue

It is finished. It has taken me a good twenty years of starts and stops, of spurts of energy followed by periods of denial, but I have finished it, the story of my mother, her history and her legacy. It has been a work of love and of soul searching. What did my mother leave me, our children and their children?

She left me with a burning desire to learn and to teach, to strive and to reach, to uncover and discover, and to give back as much as I have been given. In my eighty-sixth year I am still teaching, sixth graders and senior citizens. I teach reading and writing, yearning for beauty in the language that my mother found in Dr. Bancroft Beatley at Simmons College and President Franklin Delano Roosevelt in his Fireside Chats.

She also left me with an awareness of the senses, especially in the environment. She found beauty everywhere, and she appreciated a good cinnamon roll or a lovely piece of fabric as much as she did a beautiful sunset. I am sure she enlightened Antarctica for me as we absorbed the ice sculptures and the pristine air.

I am left with a reverence for work and for fun. When it's time to work you go all the way and when it's time for fun you give it all you've got. Life is to be treasured in all its parts. Only death and serious illness demand sadness; otherwise life is happy. I have her optimism and a bit of her humor. No one could hold a crowd like she could: a room filled with light when she entered it and all eyes were on her as she told a story, often at her own expense. I have a little of that, but I don't begrudge her that she held the patent. She gave me everything she had and I have tried to pass that on to our children.

The grandchildren remember her with love and joy and have her values: work, a full commitment to living, appreciation for beauty and a boundless love for their spouses and their children. They buy only the biggest and the best fruit, the largest melons and the biggest cookies and give unsparingly of their talents, their time and their love. Perhaps the highest tribute I can pay to my mother is that her children, the great-grandchildren who never knew her, exhibit the same qualities of loving and caring with which she filled our lives.

Thank you, Mother, from all the generations. Your legacy lives on.

About

the Author

Evelyn Lerman is a retired educator, administrator, and mediator. Twenty years ago, when she first retired to Sarasota, Florida, she continued her work with teenagers, which culminated in two books published by Morning Glory Press in Buena Park, California: T*een Moms: the Pain and the Promise* (1997) and *Safer Sex: the New Morality* (2000).

Concerned that students who did not read well could not progress in school, she wrote a curriculum based on left brain/right brain theory that she, with ten of her retired professional colleagues, has been teaching for eighteen years in the Sarasota and Manatee public schools. She has just completed *A Dressmaker's Threads,* the story of her beloved Russian Mother, a story she has been telling others for years.

Evelyn's academic background includes a B.S. in Journalism, Simmons College, Boston, MA (1947); Ed. M, Harvard Graduate School of Education, Cambridge, MA (1966); C.A.S. (Certificate of Advanced Study) in Language Development and Human Development, Harvard Graduate School of Education, Cambridge, MA (1977); Certification in Mediation, University of Massachusetts, Boston, MA (1991).